A CHANCE AT Life

How charter schools produce quality education, change the lives
of students, parents, teachers, and reshape communities

Tom Wilson, Ph.D.
Foreword by Eddie Bernice Johnson

Copyright © 2009 by Tom Wilson

All rights reserved. No part of this publication may be reproduced in any form, except for brief quotations in reviews, without the written permission of the author.

Formatting and jacket design by Anne McLaughlin, Blue Lake Design, Dickinson, Texas
Published in the United States by Baxter Press, Friendswood, Texas
Printed in Canada

ISBN: 978-1-888237-85-6

Scripture taken from the HOLY BIBLE, NEW INTERNATIONAL VERSION®. Copyright © 1973, 1978, 1984 International Bible Society. Used by permission of Zondervan. All rights reserved.
The "NIV" and "New International Version" trademarks are registered in the United States Patent and Trademark Office by International Bible Society. Use of either trademark requires the permission of International Bible Society.

Publisher's note: In some of the stories in this book, names and some details have been changed to protect anonymity.

WHAT PEOPLE ARE SAYING ABOUT CHARTER SCHOOLS:

"To promote the program, *Charter Schools — School Reform That Works*: "We must continue to innovate. We must build upon what works, and we must stop doing what doesn't work. The challenge is to take those pockets of excellence and make that the norm, rather than the exception."
—*Arne Duncan, U.S. Secretary of Education*

"Dr. Tom Wilson is an articulate, energetic, and persuasive educator and advocate who is building a network of effective charter schools in Texas and beyond, enrolling diverse students with impressive results. The story of Life School should be of great interest to parents, educators, and policy-makers concerned with improving public education in the United States."
—*Richard K. Scotch, Ph.D., Professor of Sociology and Public Policy, University of Texas at Dallas*

"Our schools don't just need more resources they need more reform. This administration will insure that every child has access to a complete and competitive education. We'll invest in innovative programs that are helping schools meet high standards and close achievement gaps. We will expand our commitment to charter schools. It is our responsibility as lawmakers and as educators to make this system work, but it is the responsibility of every citizen to participate in it."
—*President Barack Obama's Address to Congress, February 24, 2009*

"Politicians are influenced by public opinion, and they know they represent their constituents. They perform comfortably inside structural impediments, and staying at their comfort level keeps them locked into mediocrity. We must break out into new methods...new ways of doing things, and the trying creates new innovative solutions. Charter schools, contract schools, and other

ways of freedom and opportunity offer hope for better solutions... and not just playing it safe, using the same old tired, failed methods. The introduction of accountability into the Texas public school system offered an opportunity for new experiments in education. You could measure the outcomes and determine whether the experiment was working better or worse than the old way. Charter schools were an idea that probably would not have been tried without the accountability system set up prior to 1995."
—*Rod Paige, Houston Independent School District Superintendent and former United States Secretary of Education*

"Charters are an integral part of building effective public schools that prepare students for success. In many cases charters are educating students that have not succeeded in traditional public schools. Charter schools are making a real impact, providing high quality options for parents and students. Texas must do more to support these schools."
—*Tom Luce, Chair of the Texas Charter School Association, 2009*

"We must not fail in delivering the quality educational services our great state deserves. Charter schools are one alternative option available students. They are very popular with parents across the state, and urban areas are especially well served by charter public schools."
—*Bill Hobby, Lt. Gov. of Texas, 1973-1991*

"Urbanites are seeking alternative methods of education to relieve the plight of the urban poor. The challenging demographics of the late twentieth century demanded a higher quality education to prepare workers and leaders for the new US economy. [Successful charter schools] want rules that protect but not impede their growth. They have a place in the public school system to serve the educational niches not filled by public schools."
—*Lonnie Hollingsworth, Director of the Texas Classroom Teacher Association*

"Charter schools are safer than some of the urban schools, more aligned with unique interests, and provide high quality education experiences. Traditional public schools work fine in providing choices such as magnet schools and other special programs, however charter schools can supply alternatives in areas and situations where choices are limited."

—*Sandy Kress, Member, Texas State Board of Education*

I dedicate this book to my wife, Brenda Mangrum Wilson. She has been my loyal wife and my best friend for 43 years. I simply couldn't do what I do without her love and support. Brenda, I love you and look forward to many years of fun on our motorcycle rides!

"These concepts will change the face of education in this country. I challenge you as board members to support the spread of concepts offered in this presentation, and you must help in establishing other similar model schools across the nation. I believe the proposed systems provide solutions to devastating problems within our public school systems."

— *Dr. Ivor Page, Associate Professor in Computer Science in the Erik Jonsson School of Engineering and Computer Science at The University of Texas–Dallas, Guest Chairperson at the defense of my doctoral dissertation,* Texas Charter Schools and Texans Who Influenced Public Policy to Achieve a Common Goal

Contents

Acknowledgements 13
Foreword 15
Chapter 1 The Fuel of Change 19
Chapter 2 The Story of Life Schools 43
Chapter 3 A Light in the Darkness 61
Chapter 4 Back to the Future 75
Chapter 5 Navigating the Legal Waters 93
Chapter 6 Before the Doors Open 107
Chapter 7 The Spirit of the Classroom 127
Chapter 8 Steps You Can Take 143
Chapter 9 My Legacy, Your Legacy 163

APPENDICES

Character Traits 179
About the Author 183
About National Charter Consultants 187
To Order Resources 192

ACKNOWLEDGEMENTS

I appreciate the host of people who made this book possible. Deputy Superintendent Marilyn Muscanere read the rough draft and made improvements in sense and accuracy. Ms. Susanne Garner, Director of Public Relations, and her team looked through hundreds of photographs to provide pictures illustrating the Life School story, and coordinated news clippings, quotes, and copy. Ms. Debbie Kelsey, my Administrative Assistant, worked tirelessly to tie up all the loose ends. My editor and an extremely gifted writer, Pat Springle, did yeoman's work in writing, composition, and editing to bring the story to life.

Politicians often are pilloried and not praised nearly enough for their contributions. I appreciate the elected leaders who helped established Life School. Eddie Bernice Johnson, a Member of the United State House of Representatives, wrote a letter of recommendation to the State Board of Education asking for approval of the Life School petition for a charter. State Senators Royce West and Florence Shapiro are supporters, encouragers, and resources for our schools. All three public servants have visited our campuses, spoken at graduation and school events, and assisted whenever we needed help. Members of the State House of Representatives, Helen Giddings, Jim Pitts, and Bill Zelker, have represented the budgetary concerns of charter schools in the state legislature, and they continue to look for ways to provide equity in funding for charter schools. Mavis Knight, a Member of the State Board of Education, and Dr. Wright Lassiter, President of the Dallas County Community College District, strongly support Life School. The mayors of our local cities, Alan Hugley of Red Oak, Marcus Knight of Lancaster, and Ron Wilkinson of Waxahachie, have assisted us at every turn. The officials of our area have been enthusiastic partners in serving our 7,000 students and parents.

Parents have been amazingly loyalty to Life School: camping out for days to enroll their students, doing fundraisers, giving in capital campaigns to build athletic venues, being the primary educator of their student in partnership with the LS staff, and giving their time and effort to sustain the spirit of excellence in our schools.

I want to specifically thank the 32 public superintendents who work with us to serve the students of our region. I have collaborated with 19 public school district superintendents, and I'm grateful for the partnership we have with the districts in our region, especially Cedar Hill and Red Oak Independent School Districts. All of us realize the task is greater than any one district can fulfill. I am very grateful to the Dallas County Community College and the Navarro Community College Districts for providing scholarships and welcoming our students to their campuses. They provide dual credit courses to our Juniors and Seniors, who often graduate from Life School ready for their second year of college. It takes a dedicated team of committed and qualified educators to provide the wonderful education our students receive at our schools. We gladly network with them.

Finally, the staff, students, and parents are the real story of our schools. They live out the Life School story everyday, and I've been amazed at their love for learning and for each other. They make my job a pleasure, and they enrich my life more than they'll ever know.

Foreword

I became acquainted with Dr. Tom Wilson and Life School about ten years ago when I was invited to tour their first facility to observe students and teachers. Several of my staff accompanied me, and we were eager to view the workings of a new charter school in my congressional district. I found Dr. Wilson to be a dynamic individual with great passion and purpose in serving the community through the establishment of quality education.

Eddie Bernice Johnson

As we moved through each area of the school, we observed students engaged in activities. They were learning in an effective but relaxed manner. While the facility was not state-of-the-art, the building was clean, orderly, well-organized and child-friendly.

As Life School administrators shared their concern to provide better facilities, I told them, "Don't worry if your facilities aren't state-of-the-art. If you provide quality instruction in a safe learning environment, parents will eagerly support this school." Over the years as I have followed the progress of Life School, my comment proved prophetic. The school has grown from a small elementary to a much larger school that has now graduated several senior classes in the fulfillment of its mission of training leaders.

During my visit in the early days of the school, I saw an acute need for computers and technology for the children. With some connections in the industry, I helped the school secure enough computers to equip its first computer lab, and in 1999, Life School entered the computer age. It was my pleasure to assist in raising the bar for quality education and provide for children in my district.

I see great hope for the future of charter schools, and I affirm Dr. Wilson as he trains servant leaders and establishes quality schools. I am pleased to celebrate a school with a well-deserved reputation for excellence. Also, I am honored to be the speaker for the 2008-09 graduating class as Life School celebrates 10 years of serving students and their families.

Quality education is so needed in the United States that I am eager to support successful efforts wherever they are. I salute this fine school.

Eddie Bernice Johnson
United States Member of Congress
February 2009

1 | The Fuel of Change

Our greatest natural resource is the minds of our children.
—Walt Disney

I thought it would be a normal Monday morning, but the shouts and banging on the front door quickly told me this morning would be like no other.

Like most startup ventures, the first year of our charter school at Oak Cliff had been a mixture of successes and disappointments. However, we felt very encouraged and planned to expand from 266 students to 425. In the spring, we opened enrollment for the next year. In open-enrollment charter schools, slots are filled first-come first-served, and within a few weeks, we reached our cap. The last application was submitted on a Friday afternoon, and we were thankful that so many parents trusted us with their children's minds and hearts. We went home for the weekend with a deep sense of satisfaction.

I arrived at the building early on Monday morning, and I asked someone to post a sign on the door for any parents who came to enroll their children at our school. It read:

Thank you for your interest in Life School. I'm sorry, but enrollment for next year is complete. We have no more space available.

That morning, my calendar was quite crowded. I had a lot to do to get ready for the next school year, including coordinating all the work to expand our school: buying furniture, reviewing curriculum, hiring teachers, and the myriad of logistical details in order to be ready for the first day of school. My mind was already focused on the future, but only minutes after I sat down at my desk, I heard banging and muffled shouts coming from the front of the building. All our staff had heard it too, so we all converged on the front door at the same time. Gathered at the front door, we saw 30 to 35 parents who had come to enroll their children. When they read the sign, they got upset — very upset. Some were crying, and others were yelling. They screamed:

"Let us in!"

"I want my child to go to school here!"

"Surely you have room for just one more!"

"You can't do this to me. My child needs this school!"

The look in their eyes told me that these parents desperately wanted a better education for their children. To them, it wasn't optional. Many of them had been told about our school by parents of children who had attended our first year, and they heard that our school was different. These parents had learned that at Life School, children didn't have to endure substandard education and a deteriorating moral climate of drugs, violence, and ridicule. Parents of our students told their friends how their children's experiences at Life School changed their lives. Before they came, these kids had been fearful, angry, and disinterested in learning, but now they were happy and loved to go to school. For the parents at the door that morning, hope for their children's future was the fuel that drove them to insist on enrolling their children in our school.

> *The look in their eyes told me that these parents desperately wanted a better education for their children.*

I invited them to come in, and I explained that we'd be happy to accept their applications and put their children on a waiting list. I gave them no guarantees, but I explained that a certain percentage of enrolled students don't attend. My explanation gave them a glimmer of hope.

The parents' reaction that Monday morning after our first year isn't an isolated instance. In fact, something like it has become a regular phenomenon at our schools. Parents soon learned that "first-come first-served" meant exactly that, so they jockeyed for position to make sure they signed up their children. Every year, parents have lined up earlier and earlier to enroll their children. After the second year, parents lined up at 4:00 in the morning on the first day of enrollment. By the third and fourth years, they came the night before and camped out in our parking lot. Then they came two days early to get in line. Years ago, we began opening our enrollment on the first of March for the following year's school term, but in 2008, the first fell on a Monday. Our school uses church facilities, and we didn't want 200 people camping out in front of the church on Sunday morning, so we moved enrollment to Tuesday and informed parents that they couldn't begin camping in our parking lot until 2:00 on Sunday afternoon after the morning services were over.

By late afternoon, tents had sprung up all over the parking lot. As we expected, people brought their sleeping bags and grills, but they also unpacked portable televisions, computers, and every other imaginable convenience. In all, 212 tents and tarps became temporary homes for the parents and grandparents who came to enroll their children. It began as a festive affair, but March weather is fickle in north Texas, and on Monday night, a fierce storm rolled in. The wind blew a gale, the temperature dropped well below freezing, and snow and sleet pelted the area. In these conditions, "the people of the parking lot" needed help. We opened the doors of our church and invited them to come in for the night so they could stay warm. We gave them hot chocolate, coffee, and doughnuts. The next morning, they went back outside and got back in line.

We opened the doors for enrollment at 8:00 A.M., and these dear people calmly came back in the building to register their children.

I'll never forget those eventful days, but not primarily because of the weather. I recall the look of hope and determination on the faces of parents and grandparents. They were willing to endure almost anything to provide the best educational environment for the children they loved. In an interview for the Dallas Morning News, Tiffany Richey reflected on her determination to ride out the storm for the sake of her child's education. "I was warm in my sleeping bag," she told the reporter, "but it was very wet. My head was wet. My pillow was wet. Everything outside my sleeping bag was wet." She, like others who braved the weather, was invited into the church for shelter. Richey explained her rationale for camping out to enroll her child: "Our friends who have kids here rave about how wonderful it is. They apply character values in the education, and that's important to us. I haven't heard one bad thing about this school." Another mom in line, Ginger Whitman, told the reporter about her child's experience at Life School. She commented, "There's just a level of positive expectation that makes [children] want to do better. There's an attitude of excellence, and there's more encouragement that they get here."[1]

Our tent city is such a regular event each year that Dallas television stations and newspapers cover it as an annual news item. In 2008, one paper's headline read "Camping Out for a Chance at Life," and the story included photographs of people weathering the storm to enroll their kids. Year after year, we witness parents' enthusiasm to enroll kids at Life School. The year before the storm, almost 200 parents and other relatives camped out in our parking lot. Susanne Garner, the Director of Public Relations at Life Schools, reflected, "For most of them, it was a family operation. Grandparents and parents were taking turns in the line. The second woman

---

1 Karin Shaw Anderson, "Parents staking out a spot at coveted school don't mind wait," *Dallas Morning News,* March 4, 2008.

in line had called her mother in Boston telling her she was going to spend the night. Her mother thought it was pretty unbelievable that there was a school in Texas where parents would do that. Her mother flew down and took care of the kids while the parents waited in line." After she watched parents being interviewed by a Dallas news crew, Susanne commented, "The interviews showed that the parents felt it was worth the wait. The opportunity that they could possibly get their child in the school was worth what they were going through. Those same amazing parents make an amazing school."[2]

THE POWER OF HOPE

King Solomon astutely observed, "Hope deferred makes the heart sick, but a longing fulfilled is a tree of life" (Proverbs 13:12). Over my years as an educator, I've seen heartsick parents who feel hopeless about their children's experiences in public schools. They long for their children to be stimulated and encouraged in the classroom, but too often, they've watched day after day as vitality is slowly erased from their children's eyes. These parents hear stories of chaos in the classrooms, tales of teachers who are trying their best to teach but spend much of their time managing children who are misbehaving. From the earliest grades, fear often dominates the heart of a child in this environment. The thrill of learning is a distant dream — if it's even on the radar screen in the child's mind.

> *They long for their children to be stimulated and encouraged in the classroom, but too often, they've watched day after day as vitality is slowly erased from their children's eyes.*

---

2   Cited by Mandy Borgeois in "Parents camp out for chance to enroll children," *Waxahachie Daily Light,* March 2, 2007.

In a supportive learning environment, however, children flourish. Hundreds of parents have told me stories or sent letters about the remarkable transformation of their children in our schools. I met a couple at one of our parenting seminars, and they related that the environment of our school had completely changed their child in a short time. Their daughter was in the third grade, but she couldn't read or write. She had received social promotions to each grade, but she had learned virtually nothing in her years in public school. On the fourth day of class, the girl's teacher called her parents and said, "Your daughter isn't participating in class, and I can't capture her attention. I want to meet with you so we can work together to find a solution." The parents met with the teacher, and they established a plan for home and school to unlock the girl's ability to learn. Within two weeks, she was participating in class and learning. And by the end of the year, she was "commended" in three out of four areas of study because she had done so well on her state tests.

This little girl's story is wonderful and encouraging, but it is far from unique. A boy in the second grade couldn't read when he came to our school, but after a month with our teacher, he made extraordinary progress. One day, the teacher asked him to read aloud for the first time. The little boy took the page, stood up, and read the story to the class. When he finished, the whole class applauded and cheered. His teacher told me, "He had the biggest grin you ever saw. He patted himself on the back and told the class, 'I did good, didn't I?'"

When a child is struggling, the combination of early teacher intervention, parental training and involvement, and a safe, affirming classroom environment produce remarkable results — not only in the life of the child, but in the family as well. When children are happy and successful in school, the tension level at home subsides. In the classroom, children learn the benefits of respect in relationships and discipline in educational goals. They take those qualities home with them each night. Many parents have told me that their children are modeling those traits to others when they come home after school each day, and the atmosphere of the family is changing. Instead of yelling, they speak calmly; instead of accusing and blaming, each person takes responsibility for his or her behavior; and instead of settling for just getting by, they learn to set goals for a better life. And with discipline and joyful determination, they reach those goals.

> *Because our classrooms are havens of love, parents of children with learning disabilities gravitate to our schools.*

Because our classrooms are havens of love, parents of children with learning disabilities gravitate to our schools. The population of Special Education children in Life Schools is between 11% and 13%. (By comparison, most public schools have about 5%.) They experience acceptance instead of rejection, encouragement instead of ridicule, and hope instead of despair. Some years, 100% of our Special Ed children have fulfilled their AYP (Annual Yearly Progress) established by educational professionals for each child. That's a wonderful benchmark of success.

THE PURPOSE OF CHARTER SCHOOLS

Charter schools are contract schools in the public school classification of school choice options. They offer effective alternatives to traditional public education in a wide variety of settings, not only as beacons of excellence in underperforming districts, but places that provide safety and instill values in self-absorbed affluent districts. Similar to other states, the Texas Education Code establishes charter schools to accomplish specific goals:

- Improve student learning,

- Provide a choice of learning opportunities within the public school system,

- Create professional opportunities that will attract new teachers to the public school system,

- Establish a new form of accountability for public schools, and
- Encourage different and innovative learning methods.[3]

Though the state provides for several options, including open-enrollment charters, home-rule school district charters, and campus charters, educators and the public have overwhelmingly chosen open-enrollment charters as the most popular class of charter schools.

Since 1996, the Texas State Board of Education has granted contracts for open-enrollment charter schools. Some of the criteria for these schools include:

- Open-enrollment charters can't refuse admission to students within their service boundaries. There are a few exceptions to that rule, including space availability. Schools that receive more applications than available slots at each grade level must create a waiting list. When students transfer and leave slots open, the school must hold a lottery for admission.

- Open-enrollment charters in most states must be run by IRS-recognized nonprofit entities, and they often receive funding from the state based on average daily attendance.

- Unlike independent school districts, open-enrollment charter schools in most states don't receive money from local property taxes and don't receive money for facilities from the state. Some states provide startup grant money for facilities initially. The schools may receive money from private sources, but they may not charge tuition. They can charge the same types of fees that other public schools impose.

- The state's education agency may revoke the charter of an open-enrollment charter school if the charter holder violates the terms of the charter, fails to protect the health, safety or welfare of students, or engages in fiscal mismanagement.

---

3   Texas Education Code, Chapter 12, Section 12.001.

- Open-enrollment charters are granted by the state [or the local public school district] once a year. Expansions of existing charters, like those given to Life School, are often granted separately.[4]

In every school we open, we are committed to the highest standards in educational performance. Several years ago, a young man in one of our high schools was an avid learner. No one in his family had ever gone to college, but we soon recognized that he was on a path toward higher education. To stimulate his mind and encourage his heart, we explored the possibility of working with the local community college district to provide dual credit classes for high school students to also receive college credits for core high school classes — free of charge. The chancellors approved my recommendation, and today, hundreds of students, including the young man whose commitment to learning prompted the effort, have received college credits during their high school years. Many of these young men and women previously had no thought of going to college, but they find themselves on college campuses earning university credits when they are juniors and seniors in high school. You can imagine what this does for their confidence and the doors it opens for their futures. The young man who inspired this effort graduated from high school with 42 college credits. He attended the University of Texas, graduating summa cum laude in three years. Today, he is a teacher, passing along his passion for learning to other students.

> *He attended the University of Texas, graduating summa cum laude in three years. Today, he is a teacher, passing along his passion for learning to other students.*

---

4   Adapted from an article by the *Dallas Morning News*, "McKinney to have Collin County's first charter school," by Karin Shaw Anderson, January 29, 2008. Source: Texas Education Agency.

The impact of a positive learning environment certainly shapes the lives of students and their parents, but our experience shows that teachers benefit just as much. In many public schools, teachers are frustrated with the distractions, lack of respect, and restrictions that curb creativity. Scores of teachers have told us that they love teaching at our schools because they get to do what they got into teaching to do in the first place: shape the hearts and minds of children. One teacher told me, "Dr. Wilson, I taught in a public school for 13 years, and every week, I prepared five days of lesson plans. The chaos of the classroom captured a lot of my attention and disrupted the students, so I was doing well to teach three lessons a week." Tears came to her eyes as she continued, "I've been at Life School for four weeks, and I'm amazed at the difference. Students respect me and they respect each other. The atmosphere of love and encouragement makes it a delight to come to school each day — for all of us! And I've been able to teach my lessons every single day. This is what I've dreamed of for the past 13 years. Thank you for letting me be a part of what you're doing here."

Many other teachers in our schools echo her perceptions. They've told me:

- "I used to dread going to school, but now I can't wait to come to class each day."

- "When I taught in the public schools, I felt alone. No one supported me. Parents were upset with me because their children weren't learning, and the administration was angry with me because I tried to be creative. But at Life School, my peer group of teachers encourages me to be the best teacher I can be, the administration celebrates my creativity, and the parents are partners with me in equipping their children. It's amazing!"

- "I have 360 degree support in this school, and it makes all the difference in the world."

- "The vertical alignment of curriculum at this school is powerful. I know the students are learning what they need to learn in every grade and every class. That means I don't have to spend the first part of every year teaching what the students should have learned last year."

- "When I taught in the public school, I felt I was in a dysfunctional tug-of-war with parents and their child. Both of them blamed me for the student's poor performance or behavior problems. But at Life School, parents know they play a vital role — in fact, *the* vital role — in shaping their child's life, and we work together to provide the best environment for learning."

- "Instead of a teacher's job being primarily crowd control, our strategy at Life School is to 'catch children doing good,' and we reward them for living the character qualities we value."

- "Life School reverses peer pressure. Instead of children pushing each other to resist authority, lie, cheat, and commit acts of violence, they encourage each other to pursue excellence in every area of life. This transforms the entire atmosphere of the school."

- "We have a wonderful blend of a commitment to academic excellence and a spirit of celebration. We find every reason to have a party and enjoy each other, and these fun times provide a positive release for students who are working so hard in their classes."

When I assert that public schools are failing to educate our children and instill values in their lives, my indictment isn't universal (there are some wonderfully successful schools and districts around the country), and it isn't personal (even in schools that are tragically failing, we find gifted and courageous teachers who are trying their best to make a difference). But the public education system itself is flawed, and the results speak for themselves. Studies by the American College Testing Program (ACT) and the University of Chicago found that only 20% of 8th-graders are being academically prepared for college. The studies found that students' success in middle school is a predictor of their abilities to succeed in college, in the workplace, and in life. The trend was consistent across demographic and economic lines.[5] No one, even the most ardent advocate of public schools, would assert that 20% is a passing grade for public education.

Charter schools can be utilized as a tool of intervention in local districts that are perpetually ineffective in delivering adequate education. An example of charter school intervention occurred in 1995 when the United States Congress took over the Washington, D.C. school district that had been mismanaged and suffered from overt corruption. Congress created the Public Charter School Board and offered the opportunity for public and private schools, non-profit organizations, entrepreneurial educators, and community leaders to apply for charters. By 2003, 30% of students in Washington, D.C. attended charter schools.

Charter schools can be utilized as a tool of intervention in local districts that are perpetually ineffective in delivering adequate education.

A similar situation occurred in New Orleans in the aftermath of Hurricane Katrina. On November 9, 2005, Governor Kathleen Blanco announced that the state was taking control of the New Orleans public education system. At her press conference, the governor explained her reasons: "Even before the storms, New Orleans schools were not serving our children well. We cannot afford to rebuild schools that keep failing. A strong public school system is essential to a successful recovery effort. The state will take responsibility for every school in that district that is below the state average. Those schools will be placed in the Recovery School District. This is similar to what the Department of Education is doing with failing schools

---

5   Cited by Tara Malone, *The Chicago Tribune,* cited in *The Houston Chronicle,* "Only 20% of 8th-graders on track for college, study finds," A6, December 11, 2008.

throughout the state, only on a much larger scale. The State Department of Education would run those schools or find a provider with a proven record of success to run them. Among the options available to us in New Orleans are Type 5 charter schools."[6] Blanco estimated that about twenty charters would be issued to qualified entities in New Orleans. The United States Department of Education responded with grants to provide start-up funds for those schools.

Of course, not all charter schools are successful, and not all of them have the same values we cherish, but every charter school has the opportunity to draft its own set of guidelines and expectations to create the culture envisioned by its founders. I'm thrilled to work with administrators, teachers, parents, and their children who embrace these values and are seeing such wonderful results. It's a great privilege for me.

A DREAM COME TRUE

I've been involved in education for 28 years. First, I was principal of a private Christian school at the church where I was the pastor. My experience there was decidedly mixed. We were able to impart good and godly values to the students, but the lack of adequate funding led to two significant problems. We weren't able to pay our teachers as much as they deserved, and at least some of the parents used threats of not paying to try to manipulate us to get something they wanted. In some cases, they believed their payment to the school put the entire burden of supervision on us instead of on them. A few parents told me, "You'd better make my child behave, or I'm not going to keep paying the tuition. And if you don't get my money, your school will collapse." They felt like they could hold us hostage to their tuition payments, and to some extent, they were right. Our school wasn't unique. Every private

---

6 Kathleen Blanco, *Recovery School District Bill*, State of Louisiana, 2005. Cited February 17, 2006.

school administrator I've talked with over the years has told me the same kinds of stories. A few parents (certainly not all) expected us to raise their children for them, but that's not a reasonable or workable expectation.

At the same time, I was embarrassed at the low quality of education we provided at our private Christian school. We simply didn't have enough money to provide the best resources and hire the best teachers. Please don't misunderstand me. We had some of the most wonderful, kind, loving teachers at our school, but we simply didn't have sufficient financial resources to hire enough of the very best. Sadly, I was well aware that the excellent teachers at our school were sacrificing to be there. They could have gotten higher salaries at a public school, but they wanted to teach in a Christian environment. I'll always be grateful for their commitment to God and to our students, but it broke my heart to know we couldn't adequately pay them, and we couldn't find enough excellent teachers who were willing to sacrifice their income to serve kids. In our private school, I always felt that we were doing the best we could do with the resources available to us, but it just wasn't up to the standards of excellence I knew our students needed and deserved.

In traditional public schools, funding is adequate, but the bureaucracy demands inordinate time and attention for teachers to fill out reports and follow the many onerous rules demanded by state and local school systems. In countless cases, these regulations have been instituted to prevent chaos from the "bad actors" in the classrooms, but enforced peace (if it happens at all) comes at a high price: creativity is stifled and excellence is sacrificed. Conflicting rules create confusion. One set of rules requires teachers to follow procedures to curtail misbehavior and report disobedience, but other regulations are designed to protect students from oppressive and ineffective teachers. These conflicting guidelines become a straightjacket for a teacher who is trying to create a supportive, positive learning environment. Too many administrators are simply trying to avoid conflicts that could jeopardize their careers, so they follow the letter of the law to avoid being sued instead of supporting the teacher. Parents sense the teacher's weakness, and they blame the teacher for their children's poor behavior or performance.

These conflicting guidelines become a straightjacket for a teacher who is trying to create a supportive, positive learning environment.

Almost all teachers I've ever known got into teaching because they longed to make a difference in the lives of young people. Perhaps they had a gifted and affirming teacher who served as a mentor to them, and they could see themselves shaping other young lives, too. But the oppressive weight of conflicting rules, the chaotic environment of the classroom, and the lack of administrative and parental support gradually erode teachers' sense of calling. Sooner or later, their goal changes from shaping young lives to simply enduring each day, each week, each semester, and each year until retirement. Certainly, if we look around the country, we find administrators who fight against the system to provide an atmosphere where gifted teachers can thrive, but too often, public schools have more rules than learning, more fear than hope, and more jockeying for position than a commitment to educational excellence. It's a crying shame.

Through the creation of charter schools, I've gained the freedom to do education the way I believe it should be done. The charter itself, approved by the state, establishes the vision, direction, and atmosphere of our schools. A charter is a contract with the state that creates boundaries, and within those boundaries, we are free to devote ourselves to excellence in education and character development. When I walk down the halls and into classrooms and I see the looks on the faces of teachers and students, I can see the incredible impact our school is having to shape the life of every person involved. It's a dream come true for me.

Charter schools reclaim the hope for public education. Within the guidelines and with the direction provided by the charter, administrators and teachers can fulfill their deepest hopes and highest goals to make a difference in young lives. In this setting, the enthusiasm of teachers is contagious. They come to school each day as eager, prepared professionals who genuinely care about each student in their classroom. The problem in many public schools and private Christian schools isn't the curriculum or the textbooks; it's the culture surrounding administrators and teachers that prevents them from being the outstanding educators they long to be. In charter schools, in contrast, a positive culture is ingrained from the very beginning, before the doors open on the first day of class, by the prescribed direction of the charter. Cornell University professor Dr. Stacy Lee Smith observed the impact of charter schools to have an impact beyond the individual student and the school to produce a stronger society. She wrote, "Charter schools are needed to prepare future citizens for civic life. [They] fulfill public interest in democratic social reproduction to the extent that they approximate deliberative ideals — manifest equality and inclusion of all affected — within their practice of school governance as well as their civic educational practices for citizenship."[7]

Some of our students come from such disruptive homes that our schools are the safest, sanest places in their lives. And some of them have performed so poorly in other school settings that they've given up on learning. Their parents are giving our school a try as a last resort, but when these children come, amazing things happen. In our schools, I've seen children's lives change before my eyes in a matter of a few weeks. No matter what grade they enter, the love they feel and our commitment to excellence in education draws them out. If they have been withdrawn, they now take steps to engage; if they have been disruptive, they learn the value of respect; if they have neglected learning, they now sense the incredible opportunity to learn all they can so they can make something of their lives. In their insightful book, *Politics, Markets, and America's Schools,*

---

7   Stacy Lee Smith, PhD, "Democratic Public Life: Building Participatory Civic Communities through Charter Schooling," Cornell University, 1997.

John E. Chubb and Terry M. Moe observed the tidal wave of support for change in public education. They wrote, "It is time, we think, to get to the root of the problem. Choice is highly popular among ordinary citizens, reformers, state officials, and particularly governors. The power of a unified business community, broad popular support, and bold executive leadership provide an opportunity to decentralize the education system. The result will be more autonomous, responsive public schools, teachers of a higher professional caliber, and more students learning how to learn."[8]

MY HOPE FOR YOU

You may be a teacher, a school administrator, a parent, a pastor, a community leader, or someone else interested in shaping young lives. Whoever you are, I hope the message of this book inspires you to reclaim your hope for public education. Even if you don't have a position in a school, you can play a vital role to change the face of education in your community. Today, the legislatures of forty states, Washington D.C, and Puerto Rico have written laws to provide opportunities for communities to launch charter schools. These schools may be chartered by individuals with a vision, by universities, or by school district administrators who want to experiment with new designs in education. Corporations have started charter schools to advance education in their communities.

> *I believe in charter schools because they offer the best hope to change the learning environment, enlist the best teachers, partner with parents, instill values, and impart character to young people.*

I believe in charter schools because they offer the best hope to change the learning environment, enlist the best teachers, partner with parents, instill values, and impart character to young people.

---

8   John E. Chubb and Terry M. Moe, *Politics, Markets, and America's Schools,* (The Brookings Institute, Washington, D.C., 1990), p. 227.

Today, schools are failing in poor urban communities as well as wealthy suburbs. Charter schools provide opportunities for visionary educators to start fresh and establish a new environment.

Charter schools are the hope of public education. In the rest of this book, I want to give you the history of this type of school and a brief account of our experiences, and I'll offer some suggestions as you consider a charter school for your community.

Joseph Mena

In my years as an administrator at Life School, one of the most touching moments involved a 9-year-old student. "Janie" had a rough childhood. She endured physical abuse, her mother was a drug addict, and she suffered confusion and fear that would be difficult for an adult to handle, much less a child. When Janie was only 5 years old, she became the adult in the home, cooking over a hot stove and bathing her mother when she passed out. Eventually, the mother lost her parental rights, and Janie moved in with her grandparents. One day, Janie told her grandmother, "Grandma, I'm going to try and be the best little girl because I don't want you to get rid of me." Her grandmother's heart broke, and she reassured Janie that she was safe now. Her grandparents eventually adopted her. The stability of her new home, coupled with the fine teachers over these last 5 years at Life School, allowed Janie to experience the stability she needed to blossom academically and socially. Her resiliency amazes me to this day. She is a very quiet and unassuming student. You'd never guess she possesses the heart of a lion.

Every Friday at our school, I read books to the entire student body to show them the power of the written and spoken word. Sharing books can make people laugh, cry, reminisce, and draw them closer than they ever thought possible. Reading is a powerful medium. Reading allows me to connect with 500+ kids each week.

One day, I read a story about a boy who lost his dog in a car accident and how he coped with such a devastating loss. The story told how the boy cycled through shock, grief, sadness, and eventually, appreciation for the time he had enjoyed with his dog. I asked the students to raise their hands if they had experienced any type of loss, and hands shot up all over the auditorium. I encouraged them to look around and see that other students deal with the same issues. We are an extended family that supports one another through these tough times. As the students looked around, they seemed to sense that they were not alone. A real sense of "togetherness" happened that morning. It was a silence I will never forget.

After I read the story and was leaving the auditorium, I walked out next to Janie. She looked at me and with glassy eyes said, "Mr. Mena, I really liked your story this morning.

It reminded me of my mother." It took everything in me to avoid weeping at that moment because I knew the effect Janie's loss had on her.

Janie's story, though, didn't end that day. Last year's awards assembly was memorable. Our yearly awards assembly honors students for hard work, dedication, and excellence. We give out various awards ranging from ribbons and certificates to trophies for specific achievements. The "Citizenship" and "Principal's" awards are especially prized. When students' names are called, they step forward, I walk to them, hand them their certificate, and thank them for being a great example to their classmates.

That day, Janie's class found their way up to the stage and waited. The director of ceremonies announced, "And our Principal's Award goes to Janie McDonald." As she stepped forward, her smile beamed, and she immediately looked downstage for me. Her eyes were taking in every second. As she looked at me, the smile on her face lit up the room.

At that moment, my emotions got the best of me. Knowing the trials that this little girl had overcome — succeeding academically by earning "A" honor roll status, scoring at the highest level on her state assessments, and now being recognized for setting a stellar example before her classmates and achieving the school's highest honor — deeply touched my heart. As I handed the certificate to her, I somehow managed to choke out, "Janie, you have done an outstanding job this year. I can't tell you how proud I am of you." Now, I was the one with the glassy eyes. I'll cherish this moment for what it meant to Janie, and too, for the hope it represents for all children from troubled homes.

The transformation in Janie's life illustrates the very heart of Life School. We are a team of educators providing a safe, supportive environment to help children achieve their potential. The staff at Life School is second to none. I couldn't imagine fulfilling this vision and walking this road with anyone else. They help me to "live life deeply" in our commitment to our students. I will always be grateful for Dr. Wilson's vision and courage to establish a school that will have an impact on students for decades to come.

Joseph Mena
Assistant Superintendent

Kathryn Barnes

My first encounter with Life School was through a parent on my daughter's softball team. She spoke passionately about the school and the difference it had made in the lives of her children. She praised the faculty and the day-to-day operation of the school. She gave specific examples and even discussed a problem that arose in the past when her daughter was bullied. She credited the school for the manner in which the staff took immediate action and directly addressed the issue. Her enthusiasm for the school impressed me.

At the time, my oldest daughter was in a private school, and her younger sister was starting kindergarten. We were looking for a school closer to home and took time to visit several schools, charter and private. In our visit to Life School, we observed children who were obedient and respectful to their teachers. We were keenly aware of the professional manner in which the school was run. Before we left, one of the students told me (without prompting) how much she enjoyed the school. When we walked out the door that day, we knew we had found the school to partner with in raising our children.

With both of our children in school, it was time for me to go back to work. I was drawn to teaching, and I truly felt Life School was God's place for me. Being a first-year teacher was daunting, but the staff was, and has continued to be, incredibly encouraging. There is a team environment, and the goal for this team is to nurture and grow tomorrow's leaders. On numerous occasions, I have heard my fellow teachers discuss how we can reach students who may be struggling, having difficulties at home, or just need to be loved and shown attention. What a blessing it is to be part of this staff!

The kids we teach are normal kids. They have identity crises, social struggles, life challenges, and big dreams. I remember one student in particular who rarely talked and usually sat alone at lunch. I sat by her one day in the cafeteria and talked with her about school, her life and the things she most enjoyed. She shared with me her journal, which was comprised of story after story she had written. I read some of her work, and I was impressed. I told her how wonderful her stories were and she lit up. The time I spent with her changed her whole demeanor. I could see her growing in wisdom and confidence before my very eyes. The experience touched me deeply.

This little girl and all the students at Life School are so special to me, but possibly the best thing about Life School is the parental involvement. Parents at our school are proactively engaged in the teaching process, and if a problem arises, the teachers and parents communicate and take action. Life School has struck a critical balance between teacher dedication, student accountability, and parental involvement that is essential for success. Can we get better? One thing is for certain...we'll try!

Dr. Kathryn Barnes
Teacher, Life School Red Oak

2 | THE STORY OF LIFE SCHOOLS

The public school system is already so beleaguered by bureaucracy; so cowed by the demands of due process; so overwhelmed with faddish curricula that its educational purpose is almost an afterthought.
— *Janice Rogers Brown, California Justice*

I've been an educator for almost three decades. Earlier in my career, I combined my role as a pastor and educator to start Christian schools in Mesquite and Austin, Texas. In November of 1988, I became the pastor of a church at Oak Cliff, a suburb of Dallas, Texas. The church already sponsored a private Christian school, but the school was in financial trouble. The church had borrowed $75,000 to pay overdue utility bills just to keep the lights on and the doors open, but it ran a $100,000 deficit each year. Years before, this church had been one of the largest and most prominent in its denomination, but those days were long past. When I became their pastor, only 200 people still attended services, and they certainly couldn't fund the enormous school deficit each year. The prospects for the future were very grim. In fact, we contemplated not only closing the school, but closing the church as well.

The education provided by our school was exemplary. The Southern Association of Private Schools accredited the school, and we had outstanding (though underpaid) teachers and administrators. They were deeply committed to quality education for their students, but by January the next year, the financial strain demanded change. I met with the administrators of the school to explain the situation and propose changes to the budget, but they refused to give an inch. They insisted that the church continue to be the backstop to provide any necessary funds. The headmaster, a highly respected educator in Christian schools in our denomination, told me, "Pastor, either the church agrees to continue to fund the school, or the administrators and teachers will walk away from it." His demand, however, wasn't tenable for the church. We met all evening and into the early hours of the next morning, but we couldn't find a compromise solution. After more deliberations the following weeks, we realized we simply weren't going to be able to continue operations, so in February, we announced the closing of the school after the term ended in late May.

The decision to close the school wasn't a simple, emotionless act. In fact, it broke my heart. I valued the quality of education, and I saw the love poured into those students each day, and I wept when I had to announce the school would be closing. I promised our church and our community, though, that someday, somehow, we'd have a school again.

The following June, about 35 people left our church because we no longer sponsored the school. Soon, more families came, and a year after Brenda and I came to the church, we had about 600 people every Sunday. For several years, we devoted ourselves to rebuilding the church. Unfortunately, we experienced power struggles among the leadership. During its decline, some of our leaders felt threatened, so they tried to wield power over those who remained. In those early years at Oak Cliff, my task was to rebuild trust and establish strong relationships so our leaders could relax and trust God together. It proved to be a monumental task, but by the grace of God, we became healthier, and more people came to our church to be fed spiritually. During this time, the hope of having a quality school never died.

THE TRAGIC TURNING POINT

In 1993, my son Scott was our youth pastor. He was a dynamic, charismatic leader, and he did a phenomenal job of gathering young people from all around our part of the city. He sponsored sports programs, outreaches, and every other kind of event to attract students so they could hear the message of God's grace. Many of those who came weren't exactly the kind you'd find in most Sunday schools around the country — they were from gangs in the roughest neighborhoods of the city. Week after week, they came to hear God's word, and obviously, they were attracted to God's love and grace, but they walked out our doors into the horrors of drugs, violence, sex, and domestic abuse that hardened their hearts again. That year, Dallas was labeled "the murder capital of the United States," and our community of faith was in the center of the storm.

Many students, including those involved with our student ministry, joined gangs to protect themselves. Hispanic and black gangs fought vicious battles in the streets and alleys, and those who weren't in gangs felt vulnerable. They joined so they'd have someone on their side when knives and guns came out. Three students involved in our youth group were involved in tragic violence. One young man died in a drive-by shooting. Whether he was the intended target or an accidental victim, we'll never know. Two others had been friends, but they joined different gangs. One invited the other to come over to his house to hang out and watch television. The first friend excused himself for a minute, walked into another room and got a gun, came back in and shot his friend in the head. He calmly took a photograph to show the leaders of his gang. The reason? In many gangs, new members have to prove their loyalty by killing someone from a rival gang. If everybody was guilty of murder, they had a blood bond between them. That's the

> *Many students, including those involved with our student ministry, joined gangs to protect themselves.*

sinister motive that turned one friend against the other. Of course, this wasn't an isolated incident. Young people lived in constant fear that they might be victims of violence at any moment.

When I learned of these tragic and senseless deaths, I was crushed. I had come to Oak Cliff to make a difference, but young people in our own church were murdering and being murdered. When I came to the church, I had written a list of goals. Our numbers had grown, but too many people's lives weren't being transformed by God's Spirit. I had given everything I had to see lives changed. I'd preached with passion, led with as clear and compelling a vision as I could communicate, and prayed long and hard. I had knocked on every door in our neighborhood to introduce myself to people and invite them to come hear the message of Christ. But now, I was looking in the face of colossal failure. Two young men were in their graves, and another was in prison for many years. I couldn't just keep going the same way and expect different results. Something had to change.

Soon after the murders, I went to my office and poured out my heart to the Lord. All day, I prayed and cried, asking God for direction and begging him to use me to genuinely touch people's hearts so their lives would changed. Late in the afternoon, I realized I was on the floor, and the carpet was wet with my tears. At that moment, I sensed God speaking to me — not audibly, but just as clearly as any person communicating with me. His message to me that day was a calling to reach out to people when they are young children, not to wait until they are teenagers or adults. I sensed that he wanted me to focus on instilling character into children so their lives could take a different direction from their earliest years. Certainly, people of any age can come to Christ and experience transformation, but sociologists report that life change is most

> **As I thought about starting another private Christian school, God redirected my thoughts. I sensed that he was telling me to start a tuition-free school.**

pronounced when it occurs earlier in life. As I thought about starting another private Christian school, God redirected my thoughts. I sensed that he was telling me to start a tuition-free school. Although I wasn't sure what he meant, I was certainly willing to explore the concept. That moment changed the direction of my life.

FORMULATING THE NEW VISION

The very next day, I began exploring the vision God had given me. I talked to our church board, but my offer wasn't very persuasive. One of them told me, "How can we afford to have a tuition-free school? We used to charge parents $4,000 a year, and we couldn't make it. There's no way we can teach children for free." Suddenly, I realized I had a lot to learn. The board told me that if I wanted to create a tuition-free school, I'd have to do it on my own. They simply didn't believe in the concept.

A few months later, I made an appointment to meet with the leaders of our denomination at a national conference in Springfield, Missouri. They had a packed agenda, so they told me I only could take 10 minutes to tell them about the vision God had given me. In a room with theater seating, I walked in and made my presentation. I spoke with as much clarity and passion as I could muster, and after 10 minutes, I sat down. For the next 45 minutes, the leaders in the meeting communicated with me and with each other that they, too, understood that this vision for quality education was from God. Many of the people there voiced their heart-felt commitment, and the General Superintendent said, "I believe we need to support Pastor Wilson's efforts." They voted unanimously to make starting a tuition-free school a mission project of the denomination. With their endorsement, I was able to raise $85,000 to fund the development of the concept.

During the next four years, I read over 200 books to explore every educational theory and every practical possibility of tuition-free schools. In 1995, the state of Texas passed legislation to make it possible to start charter schools. When I read about it, I quickly realized this concept was what I'd been searching for. Today, you can find samples of excellent charters, but when I began writing our charter, I started from scratch. I had met and heard about some wonderfully gifted people, and I enlisted their assistance. Bob Schulman is an outstanding educational attorney. I attended his seminar, learned all I could, and I asked him to help me draft our legal documents and wade through the legal processes for our schools. Dr. Tony Picchioni was the chairperson of the state board supervising school counselors and psychologists. He gave me direction to write the elements of the charter that create a powerfully positive environment for our staff and students. Dr. Faith Hill, the head of curriculum for the Irving Independent School District, wrote wonderful lesson plans for every day of the school year from kindergarten through the fifth grade for our school. Dr. and Mrs. Gary McElhany are outstanding educators. They helped me draft the charter in language valued by the state authorities that would review our application.

I went to Austin to spend time with legislators and state educators to discover what was actually expected in an application for a charter school. In the years I had been a pastor in Austin, I had been actively involved in politics, and I knew that often what decision-makers expected wasn't necessarily what was stated in documents. State Senators Royce West and Helen Giddings, and U.S. Representative Eddie Bernice-Johnson helped me navigate the waters of state government and uncover the hidden expectations. Their support was instrumental to our success.

> **While I worked with the attorney, educators, and legislators, we built a strong coalition around Oak Cliff to show the Texas Education Association that we had strong community support.**

While I worked with the attorney, educators, and legislators, we built a strong coalition around Oak Cliff to show the Texas Education Association that we had strong community support. About 350 parents signed commitments to enroll their children in our school. I met with local government officials to share the vision, and I made a special point to meet with superintendents of schools in our region to build relationships with them. I didn't want them to see me as a threat or an adversary. Instead, I wanted to correct any misconceptions and, as much as possible, build a working relationship with these men and women. Even in those early months of preparation, we met with teachers who wanted to find more fulfillment than they'd experienced in traditional public schools. When we shared our vision with them, the vast majority indicated they wanted to teach at our school. Building community support isn't a secondary issue; it's essential to having an application accepted by the state. We had to prove to the Texas Education Agency that local community leaders, teachers, and parents supported the creation of a new, innovative approach to public education.

ACCEPTANCE AND PREPARATION

The year we applied for acceptance of our petition, the TEA received 800 inquiries and applications from around the state. Of those, only 84 complied with every aspect of the extensive application matrix containing about 50 specific requirements. A committee reviewed those that complied, and they prioritized them. Their plan was to offer charters to half of those who complied — the half that held the most promise for success. They wanted the first examples in the state to be models for the future, and they believed that starting with the top applicants would assure maximum success. Ours was one of the 42 accepted.

We received our letter of acceptance on March 8, 1998, and we immediately went to work to prepare to open our doors the following August. We quickly found ourselves in a whirlwind of activity. We interviewed hundreds of teachers to find the ones who were supremely qualified to teach at our school. We ordered furnishings for the offices and classrooms, books, and everything else we needed. The funding for our preparations, though, was a problem. Today, new schools can apply for start-up grants, but at that time, no grants were available. I had to find the money from some other source. My calculations showed that we needed about $300,000. The $85,000 I had raised in the previous years had been wisely spent on the professionals who guided us to get our charter. That money was gone. We had come so far that I wasn't going to let anything stop us now. I cashed out my retirement funds, and then I went to the bank and took out a second mortgage on everything Brenda and I owned: our home, our cars, and our furnishings. The total came to $175,000. We'd have to make that amount stretch to cover all our expenses before school opened.

The first people I hired were two wonderful administrators, Susanne Garner and Marilyn Muscanere, who are still with me today. Together, we wrote our policy manuals and handbooks for parents, our staff, and the students. We obtained copies of the discipline policies and procedures from many school districts in Dallas, and we used those as a springboard to draft our own. At the time, there were 16 charter schools operating in Texas, and we interviewed the superintendents of the ones that we felt most closely approximated our goals and values. By August of 1998, our staff was in place.

In the months of preparation when we were drafting our charter and fulfilling the state's requirements for a charter school, we had conducted dozens of community meetings to inform parents about our concept of a tuition-free, state-funded public school. Hundreds had signed up to show their intention to enroll their children, and now we contacted them again to actually enroll students for the upcoming school year. To complete our enrollment, we sent out fliers, held more community meetings, and asked parents to tell their friends about our school.

QUESTIONS FROM BOTH SIDES

At our first community meeting after we had been approved by the state, six reporters from Dallas newspapers, plus radio and television stations, came to investigate us. They knew of my background as a pastor, and they assumed I was using the school as a way to get public funding for Christian education. They were relentless in their questions, but I assured them over and over again that our school would follow the strict requirements of the law. I explained, "My integrity will not allow me to go

> *We will not, and indeed **cannot**, promote any religion. We are a public school like any other Texas public school.*

beyond the state's requirements for public education. Our purpose is to provide the finest education, not to preach or convert people. We will not, and indeed *cannot*, promote any religion. We are a public school like any other Texas public school."

The attacks, however, didn't come only from the media. As parents heard me answer the media's questions in the community meeting, some of them became furious. They stood up and demanded that we teach a Christian curriculum. As patiently as I had answered the media's piercing questions, I tried to answer the parents' concerns. I told them that I'm a Christian who has a vision for quality public education to equip our children academically and instill character in the lives of young people — but ours is a state-funded public school, and we cannot teach a Christian curriculum. One man angrily insisted, "Then we'll get together every morning to pray that you'll change your mind and teach about God!"

I politely repeated my point: "I'm more than happy for you to pray for our school and for our children, but we won't change our minds about the purpose and curriculum of our school. If you want your child to receive a Christian education, you'll need to enroll him in a private church-sponsored school, not ours."

Over the years, I've had plenty of practice explaining my role and the purpose of our school. When we conduct parents' seminars at the beginning of each school year, I tell them, "This is a public school. We don't promote religion, but we want to teach and model character traits to your children. These character qualities are valued by all religions, all governments, and civilized society at large." When I outline those traits, I've never had anyone disagree with them or insist they aren't important. Qualities such as respect, honesty, integrity, friendship, trust, hope, perseverance, and punctuality are valuable to all people in every culture. Of course, people with a Judeo-Christian worldview will recognize those character traits in the Ten Commandments, the Sermon on the Mount, and Paul's list of "the fruit of the Spirit." Parents and their children can be assured that we will actively promote their children learning these traits and living by them. At home and at church, they can use the Bible to reinforce what they learn at school, but we never use any religious teaching in our classrooms or any other school-sponsored function.

The values we impart at our schools have been shaped by timeless truths. In our schools, we've found that those truths work for people of any faith tradition. When people are gripped by those values, their attitudes and actions demonstrate their convictions without having to preach the message. Although we don't promote prescribed prayers, the Supreme Court has ruled that students can pray anytime, as long as they don't infringe on the rights of others. Do people pray in our schools? Of course they do, but never as a part of any school-directed activity. Do students speak of their faith in God? Yes, students often talk about their beliefs because we recognize our nation's basic right of the freedom of religion. Our school, however, never promotes religion in any form or fashion.

The values we impart at our schools have been shaped by timeless truths. In our schools, we've found that those truths work for people of any faith tradition.

When their children first enroll in our schools, about half of the parents of our students don't attend church. They bring their children to us to receive quality education, not to receive religious training. They appreciate our commitment to character development as well as educational excellence, and they don't have to wonder if we're trying to convert anyone to a belief system. We make our purpose crystal clear from the beginning of our interactions with these parents.

I make no apology for being a man of faith. That's who I am, and everything about me is permeated by my relationship with God. I have complete freedom to pray, but I never infringe on anyone else's choice to pray or not to pray. When I walk down the halls of our school, I pray silently for the students walking to class. When I look through the window of the door of each classroom, I pray that God will work powerfully in the lives of the teachers to love, protect, and equip their students. I ask God to make these teachers outstanding examples of the character qualities we want to impart to every student in our school. When I see parents dropping off their children or meeting with teachers, I pray that God will work powerfully to transform every person involved in the educational transaction. Sometimes, I know the family well enough to know that the student is a beacon of light in the family's darkness. In these families, the child is the parents' best hope to learn wisdom, know peace, and find love and forgiveness throughout the family. I pray that all of our students will have a profoundly positive impact on their brothers, sisters, and parents. I believe the God of heaven listens and answers these prayers.

I am fully, completely devoted to God, and part of my devotion to him is to live in integrity. That means I follow the laws of the state and honor the educational guidelines of our charter. I don't sense any conflict in my heart about this — not in the least. I am at peace about my position and my role, and I intensely pursue the very best educational experience for each of our students. Being a devoted follower of Christ doesn't mean I only communicate the gospel message verbally. When Jesus described the rewards we'll enjoy in heaven, he pointedly said that God highly values our care for the disadvantaged. Jesus explained,

"Then the King will say to those on his right, 'Come, you who are blessed by my Father; take your inheritance, the kingdom prepared for you since the creation of the world. For I was hungry and you gave me something to eat, I was thirsty and you gave me something to drink, I was a stranger and you invited me in, I needed clothes and you clothed me, I was sick and you looked after me, I was in prison and you came to visit me.' Then the righteous will answer him, 'Lord, when did we see you hungry and feed you, or thirsty and give you something to drink? When did we see you a stranger and invite you in, or needing clothes and clothe you? When did we see you sick or in prison and go to visit you?' The King will reply, 'I tell you the truth, whatever you did for one of the least of these brothers of mine, you did for me.' " (Matthew 25:34-40)

I believe many of the children in our neighborhoods compare to the hungry, thirsty, lonely, naked, and prisoners Jesus identified as "the least of these," and it is my privilege and responsibility to care for them by giving them the very best education I can possibly provide.

SOLID GOLD

That first year, the parents caught the vision, and 266 students were enrolled on the first day of class. The next year, we increased the number at Oak Cliff to 425 students, and in subsequent years, we've expanded to start charter schools in several other locations, including Red Oak, McKinney, and Lancaster. Every year, each of our schools has received a Gold Performance Acknowledgement from the Texas Education Association for excellence in student academic performance. We are

Every year, each of our schools has received a Gold Performance Acknowledgement from the Texas Education Association for excellence in student academic performance.

especially proud of these awards because they affirm our purpose to be holistic in our approach to education — promoting development in five core areas: physical fitness, emotional intelligence, social intelligence, and moral intelligence, as well as academic excellence. Our goal is to impart wisdom, the ability to apply knowledge. For example, we try to help our children understand the implications of the choices they make. For example, if they make excellent grades but have their bodies pierced and tattooed, they need to realize that these decisions may cause them to forfeit a coveted job they want after they leave school and enter the job market. Tokens of cultural identity may seem like a good idea when someone is 15 years old, but they may send the wrong message to potential employers later. We want to prepare young people for the future by guiding them to consider the long-term implications of today's choices.

When we craft our communication to our staff and parents, we want everything we say and do to reinforce our values. To accomplish this, we've come up with the acronym CAPS: Character + Academics + Parental involvement = Success. When our staff members talk to students and their parents, we use this acronym as a template to explain our purpose and processes. Similarly, when parents tell their friends about our schools, they can use it to be simple and clear about the impact we want to have on our students.

There are many benchmarks of success for Life Schools, but perhaps the one that is most memorable to the community is the Education Summit. At this important gathering, over 2,000 parents, local mayors, city council members, business and community leaders listened to a forum of State Representatives who shared their enthusiasm and commitment to charter schools. A highlight of the evening at a recent Summit was the performance of singing "God Bless America." Then 750 Life School students led the audience in the Pledge of Allegiance and with deep emotion sang the school song:

We are children of destiny, purpose and pride;
Knowing who we are with our eyes on the prize;

Determined to succeed, we'll let nothing stand in our way;
Here at Life School, a school with a dream and a future;
Here at Life School, our dreams can become reality;
Because of the strength inside me;
Because of my strength I will achieve.

There were a lot of teary eyes when they finished the song. Next, I had the privilege of recognizing staff members who have served with us for five years, and we heard from outstanding alumni who are pursuing careers in medicine, engineering, the military, and other professions. The Education Summit is a celebration of growth and achievement, and it also affirms to parents and community leaders that our schools are making a profound impact on students and their families.

The long, laborious process of petitioning for a charter and setting up a new school may, at times, seem like it's simply too much trouble, but when we see the fruit of our work in the faces and stories of those we touch each day, we experience satisfaction in the depths of our hearts. It's worth it.

Kathleen Witte

One year, a very special child I'll call John became a part of our Kindergarten program at Life School. From almost the first day of school, John's teacher realized that he would face some big challenges. He was far behind his classmates physically, in academic skill level, retention of information, and even basic social skills. He was unable to write his name or identify more than two letter names or sounds. Most of the time, he was unable to participate with the class and often caused disruptions. John sometimes got extremely upset and yelled over simple things like someone moving his pencil. When the other students were echoing letter names and sounds, John often uttered unintelligible sounds, thinking that he was participating.

Thanks to an environment that encourages collaboration and team work, John's teacher quickly asked for help from the assistant principal, her Kindergarten team and the Special Education Department. She also began to work closely with John's mother, who loves him dearly and desperately wants to help him even though she functions at low level of cognitive ability herself. John's mother heard about Life School and drives at least thirty minutes a day to bring him to school. Soon, a team was formed around John, and everyone began working hard for his success. John was placed in pull-out reading intervention group, but it didn't seem to be a good fit for him. John's teacher teamed with another Kindergarten teacher to give John the extra help that he needed in reading. His progress was slow, and most days were very frustrating for his teacher. Refusing to give up, the team loved John and continued to help him in every possible way.

Meanwhile, John was referred by his teacher and the Student Success Team to Special Education for further testing. We discovered that John qualified for Special Education services, including speech and occupational therapy. However, John's team didn't use his diagnosis as an excuse for lack of progress. They continued to work aggressively towards his success. By the end of the year, John was considered to be "still developing" in reading, but he was able to identify most of his letter names and sounds. The team decided that John would benefit from another year of Kindergarten, and this time he would be with the teacher from across the hall who had given her time to work with him and had come to love him.

John arrived at Kindergarten the following year a different child. His familiarity with the Kindergarten routine gave him confidence, and his teacher worked hard to encourage him to be a leader in his classroom. He quickly showed the new Kindergarten students the ropes. He was able to retain most of what he learned the previous year, and he continued to make progress. Although academic tasks may never come easy for John, his team searched to find different pathways to learning for him. He is discovering some coping skills that will serve him for a lifetime of learning. At his last evaluation, he was no longer considered mentally retarded, but is functioning at a learning disabled level. I believe that the efforts of John's team have changed the course of his life. When children struggle, it takes a very special team of parents and educators to find ways for them to reach their potential — no matter what the challenges. At Life School, I believe that we have that kind of team.

Kathleen Witte
Elementary Principal, Life School Oak Cliff

La Donna Bowens

When my first child was ready to start school, I was in turmoil. The Dallas Independent School District had such a horrible reputation for its educational standards that I was afraid to send my child to school. I searched the private schools, but I soon realized I couldn't afford them.

Then I heard about Life Charter School in Oak Cliff. It is a school dedicated to character development as well as academic excellence. The children wear uniforms to avoid the cliques that are so present in public schools. The parents are required to participate in the school's activities, and the school's disciplinary practices are based on a clear, workable tally system. This place sounded ideal for my child!

I went down to Life Charter School to pick up paperwork and tour the school. I met the principal and the kindergarten teachers, and instantly, I was hooked. The principal, Susanne Garner, put my heart at ease. The following fall, I sent my only child to the care of Kathleen Witte as his kindergarten teacher. I was so thankful for such a warm and loving atmosphere, and since the day he started school there, I haven't had a single regret. My second child went on the waiting list as soon as she was of age.

My son is now in the 9th grade and a daughter in 6th. To be honest, I can't imagine my children going to any other school. I have recommended many people to Life School Oak Cliff because it has a standard of excellence that is renowned in the community. Life School is the only school for my children.

La Donna Bowens
Parent

3 | A LIGHT IN THE DARKNESS

Just as eating against one's will is injurious to health, so studying without a liking for it spoils the memory, and it retains nothing it takes in.
—*Leonardo da Vinci*

Darkness in education takes many different forms, but primarily, it manifests itself in two distinct forms: pervasive ignorance (the lack of learning) and moral decay (which is seen in the deterioration of values). Sadly, some schools are afflicted with both forms of darkness. The teachers, even the best of them, have to settle for a role as policeman doing crowd control instead of instructing young minds and inspiring young hearts for the future. In many classrooms, instilling character in students isn't a goal, and in fact, some administrators, teachers, and parents may actually resist the concept of moral development of children. These school officials have been taught that morality is neutral, not the business of state-sponsored education. Popular theories of the 20th century, Values Clarification and Situational Ethics, dominate the traditional public education policies toward molding student behavior. These parents, for a variety of reasons, want their children to experience as much freedom and excitement as possible, even if this freedom interferes with their intellectual and moral development. Even in academically successful schools, excellent teachers often spend an inordinate amount of time either trying to manage the disorder in their classrooms or filling out forms the state requires for the teacher to show order is being maintained. That's not what these dear teachers dreamed of doing when they earned their degrees and certificates. They wanted more, much more.

Many public school systems are run by boards that are philosophically committed to be politically correct, that is, they avoid setting universal standards of moral conduct because these may infringe on the freedoms of some of the students. The result is that the school — and each administrator and teacher in the school — becomes reactive instead of proactive, responding to acts of defiance and disobedience instead of following a curriculum that imparts character qualities of respect, honesty, and trust. In the name of personal freedom and tolerance, students and teachers face chaos in the classroom, and if not chaos, a nagging sense of tension caused by disrespect of authority, peers, and property.

Many administrators and teachers, however, want to create a different atmosphere in their schools, and many parents want their children to be in schools that promote and model excellence in moral, social, and academic standards. That's their attraction to charter schools. When our doors open every day in every class and activity, we create and celebrate attributes of good character as well as academic excellence. The pursuit of moral attributes is woven throughout our curriculum, and just as importantly, we only hire teachers who are passionately devoted to this cause. When respect is taught and modeled on campus each day, amazing things happen. The tension level comes down, and the trust level rises. Teachers and students aren't distracted by the lies and misbehavior of others. They can concentrate on learning, and they

> *When our doors open every day in every class and activity, we create and celebrate attributes of good character as well as academic excellence.*

enjoy relationships as trust grows and develops. Of course, people are thoroughly human, so they misbehave from time to time, but we have an effective process to deal with these events. The atmosphere of respect helps the offending party take responsibility instead of blaming others or denying the problem. Charter schools aren't heaven, but they are a couple of steps toward the elimination of distractions and the creation of an environment of sanity, affirming relationships, and the pursuit of excellence. In this atmosphere, every person can develop confidence, identify strengths, hone abilities, and look for opportunities to excel.

An important ray of light in a positive school environment is the set of high expectations for every student. I believe one of the biggest insults to students is to have low expectations for them — academically, relationally, morally, and in every other way. High expectations, combined with affirmation and celebration, powerfully inspire students to push themselves to be more and achieve more than they ever thought possible. We tell students, even (and especially) struggling students: "You can be anything you want to be. Don't ever give up. Aim high. You can do it!" Students and their teachers thrive in this environment. We've seen special needs students surpass any goals that were dreamed for them simply because a positive environment helped them overcome their innate fears and sense of inadequacy. We don't spend too much time managing anger and other forms of misbehavior caused by low expectations. Instead, we devote our energies to encouragement, affirmation, and celebration of each step forward. Who wouldn't excel in a setting like that?

Our goal setting isn't blindly optimistic. That would be disheartening and counterproductive to our students. Instead, we set goals of "Adequate Yearly Progress" in each subject for each student. For example, a child may not be the most astute in math, but we encourage him that he can do better than he did the previous year, and we'll celebrate his accomplishment when he reaches his goal.

Brooke Dollens Terry, an education policy analyst, observed the positive impact of charter schools on one of the most pressing problems in public education. He wrote, "A student drops out of an American high school every 26 seconds, according to America's Promise Alliance. . . . Lawmakers outraged at the staggering number of dropouts are looking for solutions. They should consider charter schools as a proven way to address the dropout crisis. . . . After three years at a Texas charter school, students go from being academically behind to outscoring their peers at traditional public schools in reading, writing and arithmetic, according to the Texas Center for Educational Research. Demand for charter schools is growing. Last year, nearly 17,000 Texas students were on a waiting list to attend a charter school. Nationwide, the waiting list is 365,000 students."[9] I couldn't agree more. The environment created in excellent charter schools can arrest a downward slide out of school into a harsh, difficult life. Students who might have dropped out learn to respect their teachers, their peers, and themselves, and they realize they have a bright future if they stay in school.

THE TEACHER'S CRUCIAL ROLE

It is our great privilege to provide the resources for each child to succeed. Those resources are both tangible and intangible, filling their minds and capturing their hearts. I tell our staff that our role as educators is "humaneering." We are in the process of creating innovative, confident, vision-filled young men and women who will make a difference in their world. The focal point of our philosophy of education is the teacher. If the teacher is what he or she needs to be, the students will receive all they need in order to thrive. I tell our administrators that the heart and soul of our school isn't the students; it's the teachers. They are the hub of the wheel, the generator of motivation, and the motherboard of everything good that happens to the students each moment of every day at our school.

---

9   Brooke Dollens Terry, "Charter schools can help state solve dropout woes," *Houston Chronicle*, B 11, January 23, 2009.

Quality education that fulfills my hopes as the founder and the parent's dreams for their children is only achieved if the teachers are the highest caliber and receive the resources they need to impart truth and life to their students.

> *Quality education that fulfills my hopes as the founder and the parent's dreams for their children is only achieved if the teachers are the highest caliber and receive the resources they need to impart truth and life to their students.*

Obviously, the selection of teachers is crucial to our schools' success. Recruiting, however, hasn't been a problem. When teachers in public schools find out how we have constructed our schools, the respect we engender, and the excellence we pursue, they flock to us to apply for positions. Years ago, I heard a sports analyst describe the exemplary basketball programs at the University of North Carolina and Duke University. The analyst said, "Other schools have to *recruit* their players, but these two can *select* the ones they want. Everybody wants to play there." That's our experience at Life Schools.

Each principal is responsible to recruit, select, and place every person who works on his or her campus. The principal conducts the first interview, and if the person passes this hurdle, the next interview is with our Dean of Instruction. We often have eight to ten applicants for each open position, so we have the opportunity to select very highly qualified teachers. Many of them are veteran teachers who come from other school districts, but we also recruit at educational job fairs at excellent universities in this part of the state.

After an applicant interviews with the principal and our Dean of Instruction and is accepted by both of these people, the final interview is with me. By this time, applicants have proven they are supremely qualified, but I want to be sure they clearly understand and are committed to the culture of our school. The state legislature of Texas gave five distinct reasons for approving the establishment of charter schools, and one of these is that these schools are "scientific experiments" to find better ways to teach students. I explain to prospective teachers that this isn't just a job; if they teach in our schools, they are part of a grand experiment to find a more effective way to prepare young people for the rest of their lives.

I explain to every prospective Life School teacher that our schools are already a model for others. A number of superintendents have examined Life Schools and are using us as a template as they create model schools in their districts. Their administrators are shadowing our administrators to see how our philosophy is put into action. One school district adopted our methods, and in only 18 months, 30% of their schools have improved from "under-performing" to "acceptable." This superintendent is now an advocate of our philosophy and methods.

In my interview of teachers, I carefully explain our educational philosophy and describe our culture. I let them know that our efforts are already making a difference in other districts as others adopt our ways. I explain that in the Cedar Hill Independent School District, the superintendent adopted our strategy of working with local colleges to provide dual credit courses for students, and the Cedar Hill superintendent started this program for ninth graders, not just juniors and seniors. His vision was that when students graduate from high school, they would have earned an associate's degree from the local community college. They call it the "Early College High School," and they have over 100 students in the program. I love his vision!

The environment of our schools is incredibly positive, and teachers experience great fulfillment because each day they get to do what they've dreamed of doing in their classrooms, but we can't forget that others are watching us. If we succeed, we can become a beacon of light for other schools, but if we fail, we'll just be another dark spot in the education of young people. We can't afford to flirt with failure, and I want these teachers to grasp the profound significance of their roles at our schools. They are the light in the darkness for each student who walks into their classrooms each day.

In the interview with new teachers, I also want to share my own experience with them about how Life Schools began. I tell them about the vision God gave

> *They are the light in the darkness for each student who walks into their classrooms each day.*

me in my office that day many years ago, the laborious process of learning about charter schools and enlisting professional assistance to draft our charter for the state's approval, and the marvelous way God opened doors for us to start our first school at Oak Cliff. I show them newspaper accounts of parents camping out in a winter blizzard because they were so committed to their children being taught in our school, and I share with them my personal sacrifice — glad sacrifice, but sacrifice nonetheless — to mortgage everything I owned to start this school. The purpose of telling this story isn't to elicit sympathy, but to help them grasp the depth of my commitment to the principles and the atmosphere of our charter schools. Early in the interview, I can tell that people grasp the philosophy of our schools by their heads nodding and the astute questions they ask. Then, when I tell the story about the genesis of our schools, the look on their faces lets me know they genuinely understand that this isn't a job to me; it's a calling. We want our teachers to be men and women who share the same sense of devotion to the cause of rescuing young people, building into their lives, and giving them hope and confidence for the future.

MISTAKES TO AVOID

In the last several years, I've talked to countless people exploring the possibility of starting a charter school in their communities. They, too, want to be lights in the darkness around them, but too often, their thinking is fatally flawed. If they start down the wrong path, they have no chance of winning approval of their charter. Let me identify a few mistakes that must be avoided.

◆ Some wonderful, passionate, and godly leaders want to create a charter school to use public funding to teach a Christian curriculum. This simply will not, and under state law, cannot work. I applaud their personal, spiritual motivations, but they must be able to separate their private, spiritual motives from the purpose of public education at a charter school.

Spirituality is often promoted in educational degree programs, but secular universities don't espouse conservative Christian views. Instead, they advocate general spirituality, whether it is Eastern mysticism, New Age philosophies, or any other form of religion or meditation. By their nature, they avoid exclusivity, which is a cornerstone of Christian beliefs. In the 1980s, some educators introduced values clarification into classrooms. They sought to bring out the spirituality and moral perceptions they thought were inherent in the hearts of every student. They found, however, that hearts are a mixed bag of good and evil. In response, William Bennett wrote *The Book of Virtues* as an admonition to pursue character no matter what the person's spiritual perspectives might be. In our schools, we stand on Bennett's shoulders to promote character qualities in the lives of our students.

◆ In writing the charter and establishing the culture of the school, founders have to strike a balance between complexity and simplicity. Anyone who looks at our documentation will quickly see that we went to great lengths to identify and describe each element in the life of our school. Our philosophy, strategy, and practices are clearly outlined, and our comprehensive handbooks for staff, parents, and students are carefully written. Throughout all our work, we wanted to make sure everything we do is clear to everyone involved, especially parents and students. If we impressed a few professionals by writing in education-speak, the rest of our audience (our real audience) would have been confused and misled.

Grandiosity has no place in any communication related to our school. Everything we do, from the writing of the charter to our daily interactions with people, is designed to be *meaningful, memorable,* and *portable.* If we confuse people, we fail to inform or inspire them, they won't find anything that they want to remember, and they certainly won't want to tell their family and friends what they've

> *Everything we do, from the writing of the charter to our daily interactions with people, is designed to be meaningful, memorable, and portable.*

learned. The documents, philosophy, and operating system of a school must be expansive and complete, yet simple enough to understand and use. After utilizing professionals to assist in crafting the charter to speak in the language of the state education officials, it's important to change gears to write every subsequent document and give every verbal message in the language people readily understand.

♦ When charter schools fail, the cause is often traced to poor budgeting by the founders. Like any other organization involving scores of employees and millions of dollars, adequate funding is essential for the stability of a charter school. Our schools have operated in the black soon after we opened our doors to the first students. When the recent (2008-2009) financial downturn was still on the horizon, I instructed our administrators to begin examining their budgets to anticipate the possibility of lower or delayed income from the state. They examined the primary areas of maintenance, instruction, and operations, and they found ways to cut expenses by 10%. When a reduction in state payments actually occurred because of lower state sales tax revenues (which help fund public schools), we weren't caught off guard. We simply implemented the plans we had crafted months before.

♦ In many states, funding is directly tied to the required reporting system. In some states, payments to the school are based on enrollment, but in others, payments are made according to the average daily attendance. In these states, accurate accounting of students is essential. In Texas, the system is PEIMS, Public Education Information Management System. I know of some schools that have had up to 4,000 "fatal errors" when student data wasn't correct. In those states, the school could be denied payment for those students, so this error in accounting can result in a catastrophic financial problem. Accurate recordkeeping isn't exciting, but schools that neglect this area of operations suffer significant financial distress. When the school is under-funded because of poor reporting practices, the administrators can't hire enough teachers, and students suffer.

Of course, the other side of the coin is an even bigger problem. School systems that count students who aren't in attendance receive far more than a wrist slap from the state. For charter schools, their very existence is at stake.

◆ Hiring the wrong administrators and teachers creates significant problems. Some schools try to open too quickly and fail to adequately vet their applicants. Rushing this process at the beginning leads to severe problems in the classroom, as well as in relationships with parents and other staff members. Our three-tier approach for interviews works exceptionally well. Even though we opened our first Life School only six months after approval by the state, we knew hiring the right people was crucial to our success. We devoted time and attention to each position, and we found wonderfully talented, caring men and women.

In Texas, we have the right to create at-will contracts with our staff. Our careful hiring process, our commitment to academic excellence, and our obvious care for students attracts the very best teachers, but we avoid one of the biggest pitfalls in public education: many administrators and teachers believe that poor teachers "own" their positions and can't ever be fired. Whether that's true in other school districts is debatable, but it certainly isn't true for us. We don't use at-will contracts as a threat to our teachers. It's simply good employment policy. Our teachers know very well what is expected of them, and they bring their best every single day. Neither they nor we would have it any other way.

AN OCEAN OF LOVE

Perhaps the most significant aspect of a charter school is that the founders get to craft their "educational experiment" and establish the culture of the school. Life Schools began in a vision to capture the hearts and minds of children, to protect them from senseless violence, and give them a compelling sense of purpose in life. From the beginning, we created our school to impart self-respect, diligence, and the pursuit of excellence. For us, shaping character is just as important as imparting knowledge. We hired administrators and teachers who shared our values, and in this environment, we've seen lives change before our eyes. Yes, we want students to be academically successful, but we believe that they will ultimately become successful people if they are well rounded, with social, moral, physical, and intellectual acumen. All of these goals become a reality primarily because those who care for them each day (the administrators, teachers, custodians, and volunteers) genuinely love these children.

> *Life Schools began in a vision to capture the hearts and minds of children, to protect them from senseless violence, and give them a compelling sense of purpose in life.*

When I interview prospective teachers, I tell them that I don't want their love for students to run dry by mid-afternoon each day. I explain that I'm looking for men and women who have an ocean of love — unlimited and overflowing — for children. I remind these applicants that parents drop off their children each day, entrusting their beloved sons and daughters to their care. "You need to be prepared," I tell them. "You need to have your lesson plans ready, and you need your heart to be full and overflowing with love for each child when he or she walks in the door. And I promise you: if you love those children, they'll love you in return and listen eagerly as you teach. It's a beautiful thing to experience each day."

By the time prospective teachers see me in the interview process, we are convinced they have the academic qualifications to teach, but now I'm asking for more. If they don't think they have an ocean of love in their hearts for the students in their classrooms, they should look somewhere else for a teaching position. We don't use fear or anger to control students' behavior, and no matter what happens, we don't get fed up with them and give up on their progress. After I've shared my heart about the priority of love, I ask each applicant, "Are you with me?" Quite often, they have tears in their eyes just like I have tears in mine, and they nod, "Yes, Dr. Wilson. This is what I've been dreaming about for a long, long time."

Anika Pena

I came to Life School as a student from a diverse educational background, including a mixture of both public and private schools. With my varied experiences, I was given the opportunity to compare many aspects of these schools with the more recently established system known as charter schools.

The structure of our charter school created many educational benefits in comparison to public schools. For instance, smaller classes provided a better teacher-to-student ratio. For students, more personal time with their teachers results in a better learning environment, eventually leading to the graduation of successful young adults. Uniforms created a sense of equality among the students and diminished distractions between peers. And finally, because of the overwhelmingly positive feedback from students and parents, word has spread to surrounding communities regarding the success of our school. This interest has created a waiting list for enrollment each year. The fact that people choose to come to Life School produces an amazing learning environment by eliminating those who aren't interested in learning.

One of the most obvious benefits of Life School as compared to private schools is the financial freedom for educating each student. In effect, the students receive the quality of a private school education at zero cost! Also, those who qualify for the dual credit program receive a college education with no tuition expenses as well.

Words can't express what a blessing Life School has been and the countless opportunities it has provided for me and my future. Thanks to the jumpstart of 32 college credit hours by the time I graduated, I was able to finish my bachelor's degree in three years, apply to medical school, and maintain a successful full-time job at Children's Medical Center Dallas in the Emergency Room until I am officially enrolled in medical school. And I'm only 22 years old!

Thank you teachers and administrators of Life School. You provided the greatest experience possible!

Anika Pena
Life School Oak Cliff Alumna, 2004

4 | BACK TO THE FUTURE

It's time to admit that public education operates like a planned economy, a bureaucratic system in which everybody's role is spelled out in advance and there are few incentives for innovation and productivity. It's no surprise that our school system doesn't improve: It more resembles the communist economy than our own market economy.
—Albert Shanker, President of the American Federation of Teachers

The concept of charter schools isn't a new fad in educational theory. In fact, the history of this form of education reaches back a millennium. Today, charter schools are nonsectarian public schools with a performance contract describing the philosophy of education, governance, mission and vision, goals, curriculum, and business plan. They are free, open-enrollment schools accepting all eligible students up to the school's maximum enrollment. The history of charter schools reflects the long, hard struggle between the forces of governmental centralization and local decentralization. The historical record shows that when education is deemed to be failing, officials step in to guarantee minimum standards, but often at the expense of creativity and excellence. Authors John E. Chubb and Terry M. Moe observed this tension. They wrote, "The specific kinds of democratic institutions by which American public education has been governed . . . appear to be incompatible with effective schooling. We believe existing institutions cannot solve the problem, because they are the problem — and that the key to better schools is institutional reform."[10]

THE EARLIEST CHARTERS

The Middle Ages lasted roughly a thousand years, from the fall of the Roman Empire to the dawn of the Renaissance. During the first half of this period, often called the Dark Ages, systems of education were almost non-existent in Europe. Monasteries became virtually the only lights of literature and learning. Neither the state nor the church established schools to provide education for children. Subsistence was the consuming goal for the average person, and only the wealthiest families even considered educating their children. When noble families valued education, they hired tutors to prepare their children for leadership in government, social, and business responsibilities. Some tutors taught children from multiple families, and in effect, started the first formal schools in this era. However, these tutors served at the whim of their masters. If they taught an unpopular point of view, they could be fired, punished, or imprisoned.

The charter, a medieval document granting a liberty or privilege, became a formal pledge of security for a school's existence during times of societal, political, or ecclesiastical turmoil.

As time progressed and education became more desirable to more families, a teacher planning to open a school requested a charter from the state or church. The authority, secular or ecclesiastical, considered the purpose of the school, the philosophy of the founder, and the curricula. If the petition was approved, the authority could grant the privilege to assemble students for instruction. The charter, a medieval document granting a liberty or privilege, became a formal

---

10   Ibid, Chubb and Moe, pp. 2-3.

pledge of security for a school's existence during times of societal, political, or ecclesiastical turmoil. The contract guaranteed certain freedoms to the educator within the guidelines established by the ruling authority.

Later, the success of these early charter schools encouraged expansion. In 1243, the Catholic Church granted charters to Salamanca, a city in western Spain, to open schools. These proved effective and became the model for Catholic mission schools throughout Europe into the 16th century. However, the cost of running these schools exhausted church funds, and the schools began to decline. In France, the Chantries Act of 1548 provided money from the government to fund monastic and cathedral schools. Though politicians misappropriated much of these funds, the act became the foundation for publicly funded schools in France.

During the 16th century, the Protestant Reformation swept northern Europe, and leaders of the movement recognized the need for an educated population to read the Bible, which had been recently translated into their own languages. In 1524, only three years after his excommunication from the Catholic Church by the Diet of Worms, Martin Luther wrote a letter to all towns in Germany urging the establishment and maintenance of Christian schools. Similarly, John Calvin chartered academies in Geneva, and after his death his followers continued to charter schools in France. By the 18th century, religious and secular institutions in Europe cooperated in common cause to provide public education.

CHARTER SCHOOLS IN BRITAIN AND THE COLONIES

In Britain, charter schools can be traced back to Bishop William of Wykeham's establishment of the Winchester School in 1382. King Henry VI granted a charter for Eaton School in 1442, and Henry VIII, the king who broke with the Catholic Church to divorce his first wife, granted charters for some of the most hallowed schools in England, including Westminster, Harrow, Rugby, Charterhouse, and Shrewsbury. Perhaps the most renowned schools in Europe,

Oxford and Cambridge began as grammar schools and expanded their charters to become universities. Under their charters, they sponsored preparatory schools as "feeders." By the middle of the 19th century, the system required some correction. The 1868 Public School Act freed "endowed" schools from specific restrictions and established new governing bodies. To provide much needed funding, the 1869 Endowed Schools Act standardized school charters, and a year later, legislation provided for public funding of elementary schools. Of course, public funding came with strings attached, and centralization soon followed.

Across the Atlantic, the English colonies engaged in their own struggle between centralization and decentralization of schools. The governor of Virginia, Sir William Berkeley ignored the Virginia Poor Law, which provided free education for poor children. Berkeley wrote that he was afraid that the education of common people would bring "disobedience and heresy . . . and libels against the government."[11] On the other end of the educational spectrum, Benjamin Franklin wrote a pamphlet in 1749 titled "Proposals Relating to the Education of Youth," which gave practical suggestions for setting up schools in communities throughout the colonies. The colony of Pennsylvania granted Franklin a charter to establish schools. He wrote a comprehensive curriculum, and his Academy opened 175 charter schools, including the "Chartered College of Philadelphia," which became the University of Pennsylvania.

He wrote a comprehensive curriculum, and his Academy opened 175 charter schools, including the "Chartered College of Philadelphia," which became the University of Pennsylvania.

---

11 Cited by E. H. Gwynne-Thomas, *A Concise History of Education to 1900 A. D.*, (Lanham: University Press, 1981), p. 140.

Leaders in other colonies started charter schools, too. Anglicans, Baptists, Quakers, Methodists, and Presbyterians gave their blessing to new schools, and townships also started some charter schools. Some of the finest centers of education in America began as elementary charters during this time and grew into universities, including Harvard (1638), Princeton (1746), Brown (1764), Rutgers (1766), and Dartmouth (1769).

Authorities felt free to close schools without charters whenever politics or the lack of funding made the schools undesirable. The demand for control by these authorities threatened the existence of every school without a charter. However, charters issued by strong institutional authorities or governments enabled charter schools to endure, grow, and thrive.

TRANSITION: THE PROGRESSIVE MOVEMENT

Prior to the 20th century, the educational system in the United States was entirely decentralized and under local control. The cultural and economic landscape, however, was changing. The Industrial Revolution saw a major population shift from farms to increasingly crowded cities as fathers, mothers, and often, young children worked in the mills. In addition, millions of immigrants came to America from all points of the globe, especially from Europe and Asia. Under the intense pressures of industrialization and immigration, the educational system in America threatened to collapse. In 1892, a New York pediatrician, Joseph Rice wrote a series of articles for *The Forum,* a highly respected journal, on the state of education in the United States. Dr. Rice traveled to 36 cities to investigate their schools, where he interviewed 1,200 teachers and administrators. His articles outlined the tragic state of the nation's schools. His indictment of education in America incensed the public and infuriated professional educators.

Conditions in many public schools were appalling. The desperate need for teachers led to lower standards of selection. School budgets didn't have enough money for an adequate supply of books, so teachers often used singsong drills, rote repetition, and meaningless phrases to occupy students' time. The mindless and ineffective rote method of instruction was designed to retain classroom control over 80 to 100 students in each class. Rice found corruption, mismanagement, unhealthy, and unsafe conditions in many public schools.

In contrast to these ineffective schools, Dr. Rice also uncovered a few excellent schools that could become models of "progressive" education for the rest of the country. These schools were solving the staggering educational problems of a rapidly growing urban population with diverse ethnicity and cultures. For example, he noted a "progressive corps" of teachers in Minneapolis, and "competent and progressive" teachers in Indianapolis. In La Porte, Indiana, Rice saw teachers who motivated pupils to be "helpful to one another" in peer-to-peer mentoring. He praised the Cook County (Illinois) Normal School as "one of the most progressive as well as one of the most suggestive schools" he had seen. His terms "progressive" and "suggestive" show the impact of his study of European educational theories. "Progressive" implies new and improved methods of education delivery, and "suggestive" indicates that students are encouraged to initiate activity in their quest for knowledge. In these theories, decentralization is valued, and the teacher's role is to enhance the student's eagerness to learn. In his journal articles, Dr. Rice called for dramatic change in education. He stated that public schools should disconnect from political supervision and demand scientific oversight from competent professional educators. He challenged the citizens of the nation to embrace the vitality and warmth of "Progressive Schools." Ironically, the reforms Dr. Rice promoted resulted in the states establishing educational agencies and the national government creating the U. S. Children's

> *He challenged the citizens of the nation to embrace the vitality and warmth of "Progressive Schools."*

Bureau, which was, in effect, a federal educational bureau. His desire for decentralization led directly to centralization of education.

Within two decades, the Progressive Education Movement set the standard for public schools in America. In 1912, President William Howard Taft appointed Julia Lathrop as the Chief of the U. S. Children's Bureau. Her department promoted progressive education, producing a blizzard of pamphlets assuring the immigrants, migrants, and sharecroppers that their problems could be solved by effective education.

Undoubtedly, the most prolific and effective spokesman for the movement was John Dewey, who wrote books and pamphlets and gave lectures throughout the country to promote progressive education. In an early pamphlet, "The School and Society," Dewey outlined his vision for public education: "If each one of our schools is an embryonic community life . . . saturating [the pupil] with the spirit of service, and providing him with the instruments of effective self-direction, we shall have the deepest and best guarantee of a larger society which is worthy, lovely, and harmonious." After World War I, the educational revolt of the Progressive Movement had unseated pedagogical formalism. Dewey was the consummate champion of decentralization in education, but his pervasive influence and the popularity of his ideas eventually led to centralization as bureaucratic authorities attempted to implement Dewey's values and methods.

Many social analysts today observe parallels between the circumstances at the turn of the 20th century and now in the early years of the 21st century. A hundred years ago, industrialization and immigration caused the cities to become congested, and an ineffective educational system had to be reformed. Today, millions of immigrants don't come through Ellis Island. Instead, many are undocumented and cross our southern border. The Technological Revolution has surpassed the Industrial Revolution, but for millions of Americans, remarkable advances in science haven't been translated into a better quality of life or better education. A century ago,

> *A century ago, reform changed the face of education through the Progressive Education Movement, and today, perhaps charter schools can show the way to a revolution in education for millions of students across our country.*

FREE SCHOOLS AND THE REBIRTH OF CHARTER SCHOOLS

By the 1950s, the vitality of the Progressive Movement was long gone. In the 1960s and early 1970s, Theodore Roszak and other radical educators inspired the Free School Movement, a revolt against centralization. George Denison, one of the movement's leaders, observed that the title of the movement is central to its character and purpose to banish urban blight. He wrote, "Our concern for freedom is our concern for fulfillment — of activities we deem important and of persons we know are unique. To give freedom means to stand out of the way of the formative powers possessed by others."[12] Sadly, the momentum of the Free School Movement didn't last long. It dissipated by the middle of the 1970s.

In 1983, an evaluation of American schools, called *A Nation at Risk*, warned that the quality of our educational system was unacceptably low. As a sense of outrage spread, legislative hearings and town hall meetings reverberated with discussions of ways to transform education and enhance academic achievement. The reform

---

12 George Denison, *The Lives of Children: The Story of the First Street School*, (New York: Random House, 1969), p. 2-3.

movement stated bluntly that the traditional public school system had failed children and parents, and the reformers didn't trust existing school officials to implement necessary changes. By the 1990s, the leaders of the movement suggested charter schools as a means to circumvent the entrenched bureaucracy of the traditional school system and enable visionary educators to implement change.

The first modern charter school legislation was enacted in 1991 by the Minnesota legislature. Several other states, including California, Colorado, Mississippi, Georgia, Michigan, New Mexico, Wisconsin, Arizona, Kansas, and Hawaii, soon followed Minnesota's lead. The Texas legislature approved charter school legislation in 1995, paving the way for Life Schools and many others in the state. President Bill Clinton supported proponents of charter schools by calling for the creation of 3,000 schools by 2002 through the Public Charter School Program. Support from these and other key government officials proved to be instrumental in the growth of charter schools throughout the country.

Today, in virtually all corners of our nation, charter schools are a viable alternative to traditional public education. They require an entrepreneurial spirit, determined leadership, and dedication to the process of writing the charter, gaining approval from the state, and completing a detailed process to establish an effective school. These schools are, I believe, the best alternative in the struggle between the forces to centralize and decentralize public education. The charter is drafted by concerned citizens and must be aligned with the purposes outlined by the state. This "controlled freedom" provides autonomy, stimulates creativity, and attracts excellent professional educators who enthusiastically pour themselves into the lives of their students.

This "controlled freedom" provides autonomy, stimulates creativity, and attracts excellent professional educators who enthusiastically pour themselves into the lives of their students.

Charter schools aren't a new concept. We trace their history back a thousand years, yet they offer tomorrow's best hope for today's students.

STEPS TOWARD A CHARTER

From ancient times, establishing a charter school has required vision, diplomacy, funding, and hard work. Though cultures, technology, and processes have changed over the centuries, the steps to obtain a charter have remained remarkably similar. In the resurgence of the charter school movement in the past couple of decades, states have learned from one another to craft workable and effective legislation. Though every state has, to some degree, adopted and adapted the charter school legislative language used by the states writing earlier laws, each state has its own particular agencies and requirements for charter schools. For example, applicants in Georgia submit their papers to the state Charter Schools Commission. Public schools in Texas are in "independent school districts," but they are associated in counties in Georgia. In some states, local school districts can issue charters, but in others, the state agency approves charters.

The web site of each state's department of education provides the initial information about whether the state recognizes charter schools (only 10 states don't) and the process for submitting applications. The 40 states are similar in many ways, but there are 40 different sets of nuances in how the legislation is written and the details required for a charter to be approved. Individuals who attempt to complete the entire process on their own often feel very frustrated because all of the required documents aren't listed in one place, so it's easy to miss a form or two in the application process. As I mentioned earlier, in the year we submitted our application to the state of Texas, we were one of 800 applicants and letters of request, but only 84 completed all elements of the application. Some failed to provide a detailed facility plan, some didn't include a comprehensive budget, a few failed to articulate their motivation and purpose for establishing a charter school, and others didn't outline their curricula requirements. Some applicants didn't explain why a charter school was necessary in a community where public schools already exist, others failed to adequately set up their governance, and some didn't have administrators with proper credentials in education. The year we were approved, 42 applicants met all their requirements but still didn't receive approval from the state because their applications didn't impress state officials. Meeting minimum standards wasn't enough. That year, the state used a system of prioritization to choose those who were more qualified than others. I'm honored and gratified that our petition was approved.

BEYOND THE FORMS

When I consult with a founder to get a charter for a school in a particular state, I don't just look on the state education agency's web site for a list of forms. I start there, but I always talk directly with those in the agency to determine what is most important. Quite often, I find that the state officials look more closely at a few factors, and I then know I need to make sure those areas get plenty of attention. I find out who are the certified education consultants in that state, and I consider talking to those people to enlist their involvement.

The forms listed by the state's education agency often don't include some of the most important elements of the application process. Beyond the forms to be submitted, states want tangible evidence that parents and local officials want a charter school in their community. Filling out the numerous and extensive forms was, in many respects, the easy part of the application process. The real work came in contacting hundreds of parents to enlist their commitment to send their children to our school, and talking to local officials to ask for their support as the process moved forward. We asked for letters of recommendation from mayors, city council members, the school board, local judges, state representatives, the member of the United States Congress from the area, bank presidents, business executives, and community groups like the Chamber of Commerce and the Jaycees.

In most states, but certainly not in all of them, demonstrable community support is necessary for the state agency to approve a charter. Find out who are the most influential people in the community, and talk to them. Be diplomatic, and be clear about the purpose of starting a charter school. Explain your motivations and how you'll provide outstanding education for the children of the community. A few years ago, many leaders in business and government didn't know much about charter schools, and we had to answer a lot of elementary questions about them. Today, however, most people have at least a rudimentary knowledge of this type of public education. At the end of each interview with local leaders, I ask them two questions: Will you write a letter of recommendation for the school? And who are other leaders in this community I should talk with about our school?

I always introduce myself to the local superintendents and explain that I plan to start a charter school in the community. In the vast majority of cases, state officials are very supportive of charter schools, but local school leaders are much more hesitant because they see contract schools as competition. Don't shy away from interacting with these local school leaders. If you fail to connect with them, they will be much more likely to oppose your efforts. But if you build relationships with local superintendents,

> *At the end of each interview with local leaders, I ask them two questions: Will you write a letter of recommendation for the school? And who are other leaders in this community I should talk with about our school?*

they may not actively support you, but they probably won't oppose you. When I meet with these men and women, I tell them plainly about our plans for a charter school. I don't mince words, and I don't equivocate in the least, but I don't have a demanding, condemning attitude. I ask the superintendent for advice: "I care about this community and these students, and I know you care about them, too. I'm interested in what you would do if you wanted to start a charter school. You've been here a lot longer. What advice would you give me about how we can be successful in this community?"

During the application process, the state will contact local superintendents from the 10 to 12 districts surrounding the community, perhaps those within 25 miles of the site where you hope to launch a school, to ask for their input about the charter school you plan to establish. And during the process, there will be public hearings so that parents, the school board, business leaders, and any other citizen can voice their opinions of a new charter school in their community. If you haven't talked with these people, they may come with misconceptions, and they may voice resentment that could cloud the minds of others in the room and turn the state agency against approval of your application. If, however, you have won friends in talking with these people, they will stand up for you. And if you have at least mollified those who might have been opponents, they will give tacit approval instead of resisting your efforts.

Let me be perfectly honest about this crucial point. Some people who come to me for help as they apply for a charter think that the effort to connect with community leaders can be cut short. When I tell them about all the work that is required, they sometimes shake their heads and think I'm exaggerating. I'm not. Filling out forms is only one part of the requirements to win approval from the state.

> ***Building relationships and enlisting community support is just as crucial as the raft of documents submitted to the state agency.***

Building relationships and enlisting community support is just as crucial as the raft of documents submitted to the state agency. The decision-makers in the state education agency look to local officials and other influential citizens to determine if the applicant has the support necessary for a successful school.

I'm certainly not saying that the paperwork submitted to the state isn't important. It's crucial, but it's not enough. When we applied for our charter, our documentation of motivation, values, governance, facilities, curricula, faculty, and leadership credentials was extensive and carefully proofed to make sure it impressed those who reviewed it. But from talking to state officials, we realized community support would be the tipping point for approval. I can't tell you why we were in the top half of those who passed the review process, but my strong suspicion is that the strong support we garnered from leaders in our area put us over the top. Growing a fine garden isn't accomplished in a few minutes with only a few seeds and a little sweat. It takes diligence and expertise. Doing only the minimum — in gardening and in applying for a charter school — won't win the prize.

GET THE HELP YOU NEED

I admire people who are do-it-yourselfers. They may not know how to fix a leaky pipe or a broken spoke on a bicycle, but they figure it out. They are patient and persistent, and they almost always get the job done. I know some people who seemingly can fix anything that's broken. Applying to the state for a charter, however, isn't like this. If you try to fix a broken lamp and break a piece of the assembly, you can go to the hardware store and buy a replacement. It's a little time consuming, but it's not a big deal. If you try to apply for a charter and fail, however, you will have spent thousands of dollars and months of time, and you may have disappointed countless people who have dreamed of the school opening in the town or city.

When I investigated the process of applying to the state for a charter, I enlisted the involvement of some of the most skilled and experienced professionals in the state. These gifted, dedicated men and women guided me through the labyrinth of requirements

— written and unwritten. With their assistance, we succeeded in winning approval and opening our school. These professionals gave me insights I didn't even know I needed, answered questions I didn't even know to ask, and patiently walked with me through every step of the process.

Hiring professionals costs money, but in my opinion, it's money well spent. My time is too valuable to wander around hoping I get it right the first time, and the lives of children in our community are too important for me to make mistakes that might jeopardize their futures.

Centuries ago, charter schools came into existence when caring adults had a vision to craft educational excellence for children in their community. To provide the freedom and resources they needed, they made a contract with the state or church. With the structure of that contract, teachers and administrators devoted themselves wholeheartedly to the children they taught. Today, those who launch charter schools have the same motivation, the same purpose, and the same goals to provide outstanding education for the children they love.

Eric Wurster

I remember some wonderful experiences in my second year teaching at Life School in Oak Cliff. I had just become an ESL (English as a Second Language) teacher, and therefore, I taught students who spoke languages other than English. As we got to know each other on the first day of school, I learned that I had children from around the world. The countries represented were Brazil, Guatemala, Argentina, Guinea, Mexico, and of course, America. The students spoke Portuguese, Spanish, and French. I'm sure my head was spinning as I started to wonder how I was going to make this work, but I knew I had the backing of my fellow teachers and the administration.

As that first week went on, I remember a great sense of warmth wrapping itself around the room, even though the children and I were still trying to adjust to one another. I knew that Life School was the right place for this to happen! In the first few weeks, I had a boy who was extremely intelligent, but he only spoke Portuguese. He was the only one that spoke this language, so it was a confusing time for him. He sometimes got very frustrated. For a while, he broke down and cried on a daily basis. To my surprise, there was a girl in his group who encouraged him by giving him a hug. She assured him it would be all right. He struggled for the first few weeks, but slowly, he began to pick up English, and by the end of the year, he passed many of his classmates in his grades. Those first few weeks, though, were critical to let him know that Life School was a safe place. Once he felt safe, his learning took off.

I also recall another young boy from Africa. I can picture several times when his smile simply melted my heart. In contrast to the boy from Brazil, it seemed as though he made instant friends. Slowly, he picked up English, and in short phrases he expressed his excitement in what he had done in art or gym class. His excitement for learning grew each day. Each lesson and skill brought a smile as he and I reviewed his studies. Every teacher and child he came in contact with let him know he was welcome and safe. Once again, I witnessed the loving, supportive atmosphere that allowed him to flourish and grow.

As we went through the year, a beautiful richness was evident in our studies because of these children and their unique experiences. Many schools have a variety in nationalities, but Life School has a purpose to wholeheartedly embrace these children. That special year showed me that teaching is never just about teaching, but it's also about experiences and world enrichment!

Eric Wurster
Teacher, Life School Red Oak

5 | Navigating the Legal Waters

But of all the views of [universal education], none is more important, none more legitimate, than that of rendering the people the safe, as they are the ultimate, guardians of their own liberty.
—Thomas Jefferson

A charter is a legal contract between a state's education agency and the trustees of the school. Though charter schools have a long and rich history, the recent interest in this form of public education has required extensive new legislation in every participating state. My doctoral dissertation focused on the process of crafting this legislation in Texas, and to my knowledge, only two similar studies exist in the nation. The academic world needed a clear, concise outline of the legislative process. My dissertation, published 2006 in association with my Ph. D. in Public Affairs, provides an historical perspective from the 11th century to the present on how charters empower educators to teach without interference.

When we opened Life School in 1998, states that were "early adopters" had already followed Minnesota's lead. In only seven years, they had written their own legislation to create charter schools. States who were "late adopters" stood on the shoulders of those who had pioneered this effort. Florida and California, with their large Hispanic populations, were very eager to try the experiment of charter schools to see if they could more effectively teach this relatively homogeneous population of students. These states have become leaders in the movement.

Increasingly, state legislatures see charter schools as an effective solution to the problems facing public education. After legislation passed the Texas legislature, I asked Texas Book Industry lobbyist Joe Bill Watkins why he thought the legislature was eager to pass the bill. Mr. Watkins stated five specific reasons: the public's general dissatisfaction with traditional public schools, the vast amounts of money spent in public schools with little improvement to show for it, the public's insistence on school choice, educators seeking more freedom and less bureaucracy, and the entrepreneurial spirit of Texans who believe that local leaders can provide better education for their students. In this chapter, I want to highlight a few salient points I've learned about state legislation and the legal system related to charter schools.

OUTSIDE THE SYSTEM

Perhaps the most important and revolutionary aspect of charter schools is that they are part of the public education system, but in important ways, they operate outside the system. The charter gives the trustees and superintendent freedom to establish clear, compelling values and to hire administrators and teachers who impart those values to the students. I've heard public school officials insist that teachers in their districts "own" their jobs, and no one can take them away without pursuing legal action. Whether this is true or not is a matter of debate, but it is certainly the perception of many administrators and teachers. This sense of entitlement, coupled with muddied values and

> *The charter gives the trustees and superintendent freedom to establish clear, compelling values and to hire administrators and teachers who impart those values to the students.*

chaotic classrooms, drains vision and energy from even the noblest teachers. Instead of coming to school each day full of joy and enthusiasm at the prospect of shaping young lives, they begin to dread each day, hoping to survive each year, each week, and each class each day. Certainly, this picture of teacher despair isn't universal, but it's far more common than many people might think.

The legal documents for charter schools change this equation and provide a foundation for a revolution in education. I'm sure there are some charter schools that have drifted back into complacency and mediocrity, but most have assertively pursued a life-changing blend of academic excellence and character development in a supportive, loving environment. Without the state policies and legislation to sanction them, charter schools wouldn't be possible.

RESEARCH STATE LAWS

In the early days of considering the creation of a charter school, prospective founders need to research their state's laws. The education agency of most states contains this information, but it's not necessarily easy to obtain. For instance, one state has 900 to 1,000 pages of legislation and policies regarding charter schools, but many of these are imbedded in other legislation. Unfortunately, many states' educational web sites aren't well organized. It takes someone with the skills of an archeologist and a detective to dig through all the existing legislation and uncover the pertinent documents. An uninitiated and inexperienced person searching for the first time can become hopelessly lost, at least until he learns through trial and error or finds someone to guide him.[13]

---

13   Note: I wrote my dissertation on the Texas legislative process to pass the laws regarding charter schools. Those who are interested in starting a school today may be interested in the genesis of the legislation and the people who made it possible, but this chapter is not about that initial set of laws. This chapter is designed to provide insight and direction about how to use the existing legislation and conform to its requirements.

In Texas, the legislature sits in session every two years. When they pass laws, the new legislation often overlaps previous laws and sometimes contradicts them. A few years ago, I sat on a committee tasked to blend current and past legislation regarding charter schools. We created a manual to interpret new laws in light of contradictions with the laws already on the books. At every point, we wrote guidelines to provide clarity where there was confusion and direction when laws contradicted each other. Other states have similar manuals interpreting new legislation.

Navigating the legal waters includes understanding the laws passed by the national government. In recent years, the federal government has launched new initiatives to reform existing schools and open other doors in education. President George W. Bush's initiative, No Child Left Behind, is a policy for all schools, including charter schools, to set minimum standards of performance at grade levels. President Barack Obama indicated that he intends to allocate half his promised billion dollars of additional funds for education to charter schools, even though at his inauguration only 2% of students in public school were charter school students. In an op-ed article in the *New York Times,* columnist David Brooks observes, "Obama's aides point to his long record on merit pay, his sympathy for charter schools and his tendency to highlight his commitment to serious education reform."[14] Funding, of course, always has strings attached, but charter school entrepreneurs need to carefully evaluate every opportunity to provide the best resources for students.

State legislation paves the way for charter schools to receive the same preferential treatment as traditional public schools in building facilities and receiving permits from local authorities. Many local governmental agencies, however, need to be informed that charter schools should receive this treatment. For instance, when a public school needs to expand facilities to accommodate more students for the coming year, local planning and zoning boards put the plans on

---

14 Cited in *The Houston Chronicle,* December 6, 2008, B-9.

a fast track for approval. When we needed to expand, the planning and zoning board initially put our request in line behind many others. To get the same preferential treatment other schools enjoy, I had to diplomatically inform the board that ours is a public school with the same state provisions as any other public school in the city.

FIND THE RIGHT ATTORNEY

In the earliest days when I was researching our charter, I talked to officials in the Texas Education Agency and asked them for advice. One of the most important pieces of advice they gave me was to hire the attorney who helped them write their legislation to create charter schools. His name is Bob Schulman. They told me that he's the best education attorney in the state, but he seldom takes new clients because his caseload is always full. I didn't presume my good looks and charm would sway him. Instead, I found out that he teaches seminars on the legal issues surrounding public education, and I signed up. I attended the seminar with 25 others, and I asked plenty of questions. At that point in his career, Bob didn't have much experience in working with charter schools, but I could tell that he was an excellent attorney, and I wanted him on my side.

> *One of the most important pieces of advice they gave me was to hire the attorney who helped them write their legislation to create charter schools.*

Having made a personal connection with him at the seminar, I called Bob a week or so later to ask him to be the attorney for Life Schools. As I expected, he said he was too busy, but I was persistent. I reminded him that I had attended his seminar, and he remembered me. Then I explained, "Mr. Schulman, we are trying to serve the students and parents in our community by providing the finest educational experience, and I need your help to do it right."

To frighten me off, he told me how much he charges per billable hour, but I didn't flinch. "That'll be fine," I told him. "We'll be happy to pay it."

He agreed to represent us, and I can honestly say that I can't imagine a better partner than Bob Schulman. His exemplary legal expertise is matched by his genuine care for children, and he pours his heart into the work of every client. His help didn't end when we received approval for our first charter. Bob has been our attorney at every juncture in the history of Life Schools: whenever we need to build additional facilities, open a new school, or have any questions about legal matters. Because he worked closely with the state to craft legislation, he has built relationships with officials in every corner of state government. The trust Bob has earned from state officials has paved the way for us in countless ways.

When we deal with local officials to open a school, Bob often finds himself in the role of a teacher to inform them about state regulations for charter schools. Bob can readily cite specific paragraphs of the Texas Educational Code of Law because he helped write it. With his explanations to the local officials, any confusion is quickly cleared up so that progress can continue toward a new school. For example, we chose the busiest corner in the city for one of our schools, but a city official told us that traffic would be too congested for a school at that site. Bob cited the regulation providing for public schools to be located in virtually all zoning. We wanted high visibility in the community, and we answered all the questions about ingress and egress from our facilities at the busiest hours of the day. Our school is now open at that location.

As I look back, I realize that I could have chosen any of several available attorneys, but I began by asking the officials in the state education agency who they recommended. Their advice to ask Bob Schulman was as good as gold.

STUDY THE SERVICE MANUALS

To facilitate compliance, a guidance manual often accompanies a new law to interpret aspects of the legislation. My experience on the committee helping to draft the guidance manual for a particular piece of Texas legislation demonstrated how these manuals are written. The attorney for the Texas Education Agency met with us to explain the nuances of certain parts of the new legislation and the way we needed to deal with contradictions with previous laws on the books. In some cases, we examined some particularly confusing elements, and he said, "That's a gray area." We offered our recommendations, and he gave us his advice about how to clarify the conflicting points.

State politics isn't a clean, neat process. In fact, it's very messy. In his book, *Agendas, Alternatives, and Public Policies,* John Kingdon identified the "garbage can" model of creating public policy. (A few idealistic analysts believe lawmakers form legislative policies by bringing concepts and putting them together in a neat, orderly way, like the "Tossed Salad" model. I haven't found that model functioning in the states where I've worked and consulted, but it's a pleasant idea.) Kingdon described the forces driving the agendas of lawmakers and determining the success of proposed legislation. He conceives legislators and lobbyists tossing concepts into a receptacle over a period of months or years. Later, when a problem is clearly identified, legislators can sift through all the concepts and pull out the ones that fit the problem and the solution. In this way, contributors voice different perspectives on the problem and offer a variety of solutions, or they may offer solutions to parts of the problem. The key moment is the point of connection between politics and policymaking, a point Kingdon calls a "window of opportunity." This awkward and convoluted process is always messy (hence the name of the model), but surprisingly, it works effectively. Virtually every piece of legislation in local, federal, and state governments is a product of the "garbage can" approach. The results are never perfect, but they are usually workable. This model provides a theoretical explanation for educational problems and the possibility that charter schools can be a viable solution for legislatures to solve the problems in public education today. When he reflected on the state laws enacted in Texas that approved the process to establish charter schools, Bob Schulman observed, "The process of making laws is not exact. You don't get what you went in with. I agree with Kingdon that a proposal is amended, changed, adapted, ignored, merged with another law, and so on. Sometimes you get something passed, but most of the time you don't. If it's approved, the person originating the proposal is happy to get part of what was asked for. It's a way of life in Texas politics. That's reality. That's the way it works." I'd only add that this is the way it works in every sphere of government.

Those who want to understand state law and compliance factors for charter schools need to remember that behind the language of the legislation is a power struggle between the forces of centralization and decentralization. Advocates for centralization often use reforms to remedy corruption and inefficient operations in traditional public education. Other reforms are intended to provide freedom to the professional educator attempting to achieve academic excellence. These competing reform processes create tension. Excessively centralized control constricts the creativity and motivation of administrators and teachers. In addition, the massive amount of paperwork associated with restraining the wide range of potentially harmful behavior by a school district's "bad actors," and the ineffective practices perpetuated by poor teachers, impede professional educators in pursuit of excellence. Strict regulations are designed to address the flaws of inadequate teachers and administrators, but these regulations often produce unintended negative consequences. Since the 1970s, public discussion has debated whether centralization (additional control over educators) or decentralization (freedom for educators) provided the best opportunities for

> *Those who want to understand state law and compliance factors for charter schools need to remember that behind the language of the legislation is a power struggle between the forces of centralization and decentralization.*

improvement of public education. The debate continues, and as charter schools prove to be successful, tension between the two may intensify.

Guidance manuals are designed to clean up the mess sometimes made by the "garbage can" approach to legislating state laws. If people don't understand how laws are written, they might be confused and, to be honest, quite frustrated by the inconsistencies and contradictions between laws dealing with the same issue. Knowing how laws are written provides understanding and patience, two traits that often prove vital in the process of wading through legislation and corresponding guidance manuals.

USE YOUR ATTORNEY AT EVERY TURN

Establishing a successful charter school requires consummate legal skill throughout the process, when the charter is being written and to handle legal matters every year the school is operating. A competent attorney will help pave the way for state approval of the charter, and he will assist in negotiating the myriad of local legal issues regarding constructing facilities, employment contracts, leases, and all the other matters a school faces.

Entrepreneurs are visionaries who genuinely believe they can make a difference in the world. Their strengths of passion and self-reliance, however, can lead them into deep trouble if they rely on their own abilities to handle complex legal matters. If charter school founders are tempted to try to save money by not hiring or delaying the hiring of an attorney, I strongly advise them to reconsider. Hiring an excellent attorney and a competent consultant are the best expenditures a founder will make in establishing a charter school.

Navigating the legal waters to start a charter school can be complex and confusing, but don't give up; others have successfully found their way. Find those who have been successful, and learn all you can from them. Ask state officials for advice to discover the best legal minds in the state, and hire a gifted, experienced attorney who genuinely cares about children and wants your school to succeed. Above all, don't let the myriad of state demands and the piles of papers cause you to despair. Remember why you are interested in founding a charter school. Keep the vision of quality education in front of you every day. When you think of the children and the way your school will change their lives, you'll stay motivated to keep moving forward toward your goal.

Bob Schulman

A HYBRID OF THE FUTURE

It's a bird . . . it's a plane . . . it's a corporation . . . it's a government!

What in the heck is it? Well, son, it's a Texas open-enrollment charter school. You see, charter schools are really public school systems that have been created by special laws. They possess most of the attributes of a governmental body. A non-profit corporate board governs charter schools, but they are regulated as if they were public school systems. And just like automobiles, there are some good efficient ones and there are some gas guzzlers. And some are the modern hybrids on the highway of education. Life School is the latter.

Dr. Tom Wilson understands the public role played by charter schools and knows how to blend it with a business model without diluting public purpose. He is aware that in founding the charter school movement, the Texas Legislature clearly declared that open-enrollment charters are members of the public school system of the state. He has also had firsthand experience in observing that the public purpose and public nature of charter schools are often misunderstood and misinterpreted by others. Sometimes the others are well-intentioned but misinformed representatives of public agencies who, at best, would treat charters as if they were second-class, profiteering institutions, and at worst, as a pariah, to be shunned and avoided at all costs.

Such was the case with a local municipality, which just days before a new school year was to commence issued an edict intent on preventing a brand new Life School campus from opening its doors. Only months before, the same municipality was determined to deny a building permit to this very campus. In both instances, it was obvious to me and to all the Life staffers that the municipality would have responded differently if the campus in question were from a school district and not a charter school.

I can report that in both instances the municipality in question was convinced to permit the campus to open and operate. However, the negotiations were continuous and intense, and the officials were not easily convinced. Merely holding up the law to these officials was not enough. In the end, on both occasions it took a team of professionals to turn the corner. This assemblage of professionals — whom Dr. Wilson appears to select on the basis of character, skills and experience — is in my opinion the most significant attribute separating Life School's highly successful schools from the others, and this gathering of professionals makes Life Schools a hybrid of the future.

Bob Schulman
Education Attorney

6 | BEFORE THE DOORS OPEN

When it comes to education, we should never be afraid to try a new idea.
—Bob Bullock, Texas Lieutenant Governor, 1991-1999

Charter school founders are visionaries. Long before the first day their schools open, they often close their eyes and imagine eager students in the halls and educators teaching in well-ordered classrooms. I wish it were that immediate and effortless. The reality is that the completing the application process and opening the doors for the first day of class is long and arduous.

The process of applying to the designated education agency includes drafting all of the elements of the petition, addressing issues from values to governance, and from faculty to facilities. The founders probably won't receive approval unless their plans have been concrete and specific. State agencies or school boards aren't interested in ethereal notions of what a school might become; they demand specificity and details of every element of the plan. For example, they aren't impressed by the intention to find a facility after approval. They want to see photographs of an actual building, including proposed traffic patterns, floor plans, and details that prove the applicants have a viable property for the school. The building may not be under contract yet, but it must be available with a letter of intent for the school to use it.

KEY INGREDIENTS

Before the application is submitted to the state, most applicants take a year and a half to two years to establish a governing board, prepare all the documentation, craft policies, find prospective administrators and teachers, sign up parents who want their children to attend the school, and build relationships with officials in the community.

On the day the petition for a charter is approved by the commissioner and/or the state board of education, a new wave of preparations begins. In many ways, the school has already been created on paper in all of the elements of the petition for the charter, but now all of those concepts and plans have to be put into effect before the first students walk through the doors.

If they are determined and energetic, founders can open a school in six months from the time the petition is approved. We were approved for our first school in March, and our first day of classes was in August. Some founders, however, take an additional year to prepare for the first day of classes. No matter how long it takes, a number of steps must be taken for the new school to be ready for students.

Hire top administrators.

The person who is tasked to pull everything together is probably the same one who had the initial vision for the school and orchestrated all the elements of the petition. This person may be called the founder, the chief executive officer, the principal, or the superintendent. The charter identifies the nomenclature of the school's officials. If they plan to call the school an "academy," they may prefer the title of "headmaster" for the top administrator. I was (and remain) the superintendent for Life Schools.

The first action I took after we received approval for our first school was to hire two administrators, a principal and an assistant principal, to assist me in handling the myriad of details and working with the host of volunteers during the six months before we opened. They were with me in the office every day. Could we have used more salaried employees during that time? Of course, but we didn't have the resources to hire any more. For

> *The selection of those two top administrators was of paramount importance.*

that reason, the selection of those two top administrators was of paramount importance. As you may recall from an earlier chapter, I had borrowed as much money as possible to fund the start up of the school. I didn't take a salary during this transition, and we had to use every dollar judiciously.

The founder and these key administrators construct a timeline of dates, decisions, meetings, and other important events. With a small staff, adequate planning is absolutely essential. A school can't be started "by the seat of your pants." Carefully orchestrate the plan, schedule, budget, and people who are responsible for each element delivered in the process. Undoubtedly, unanticipated difficulties and unexpected delays will occur, but a comprehensive, workable plan will help these visionary leaders be ready on Day One.

Apply for tax-exempt status.

Most states require the non-profit that sponsors a new charter school to obtain tax-exemption from the Internal Revenue Service. In these states, one of the first tasks of the founder and the attorney is to apply for a 501c3 non-profit status for the school. The approval process with the IRS takes about six months (and often longer — so it's wise to apply immediately after receiving approval of the petition for the school), and upon approval, an organization remains on probationary status for three years. When the tax-exemption is approved, the school can raise money through donations. A few states allow for-profit companies to start charter schools, but this is increasingly rare.

Enlist volunteers.

We simply could not have opened Life School without the hard work and passion of fifty or sixty men and women who were dedicated to the cause. These people caught the vision for our school, and they gave their time and energy to do whatever it took to make it successful. Many of our volunteers were parents who planned to send their children to Life School. Our small administrative staff organized them into teams and gave direction to their efforts. We also found educators who spent their free time to help us because they wanted to provide a quality school for their community. If a founder's vision is clear and compelling, people come out of the woodwork to help. On the first day of classes when the doors opened, these volunteers felt just as thrilled as I did because they had invested so much in our school.

Secure the facilities.

The enrollment caps for each grade level determine the scope of the facilities required for the school. State law stipulates that enrollment is first-come first-served, so when the cap is reached, enrollment is closed (except for a waiting list).

Most new schools have to renovate existing facilities or build out spaces that weren't originally designed as school buildings. Public schools require compliance with the guidelines for public access, including facilities for people with disabilities according to the Americans with Disabilities Act (ADA). As any developer and builder can attest, getting city approval for major projects can be a nightmare. Your attorney will guide you through this process and represent you when necessary. If you haven't built relationships with city and public works officials during the application process,

If you haven't built relationships with city and public works officials during the application process, demanding quick action now may prove to be counterproductive.

demanding quick action now may prove to be counterproductive. Delays, even in the most advantageous circumstances, are almost inevitable, so start soon, hire competent and diplomatic contractors, and don't be surprised when city officials require you to jump through additional hoops to get permits and approvals.

In our experience opening schools, I'd estimate that we had to work with 18 to 30 different city departments and vendors, such as planning and zoning, traffic flow, phone, water and sewer, electricity, security, and information technology. The web of requirements was so extensive that we hired a retired contractor to untangle all the threads for us. His experience and expertise proved invaluable. Public schools often have a year after they open to comply with at least some of the regulations. Even if the facilities don't fully conform, however, the school must make accommodations from the first day for handicapped or disabled people on campus. The principle is that charter schools are public schools, so whatever is required or waived for a traditional public school is similarly required or waived for a charter school.

In recent years, public schools have made great advances in technology, not only as resources for students, but also to fulfill reporting requirements to the state. Founders and administrators can investigate companies that offer phone and Internet services to find the most reliable and cost-efficient service available in the area.

Security measures at charter schools are very important. Our campuses are locked, so no one has access to our campuses without being screened and approved. Examine the security policies and procedures of similar schools in your state to determine the best way to protect your students.

In some cases, the problem in getting permits and approvals from the myriad of city officials doesn't come simply because they are overloaded with requests; it's because they don't want a charter school to open. Their perception is that life would be easier if we didn't open our school. They wouldn't have to do the additional work of processing our request, and unless they've caught the vision for the difference we can make in students' lives, they don't see any reason for us to exist at all. They wished we would just go away, and they see us as an annoyance. I can understand their point of view. For example, the police departments already have enough to worry about without adding another school to their city. When we open a school, we might have 2,000 cars coming to our facility each day. That's a headache they don't want! Our solution is to introduce ourselves to the police chief and his lieutenants during the months of due diligence before we receive approval for our charter. We offer to employ their officers as off-duty security. We share our vision and help them understand the purpose for our school. We hope they become enthusiastic advocates for us, but if not, at least they won't actively resist our efforts.

Before we opened one of our schools, a number of city staff dragged their feet on a host of approvals. The mayor and other top city administrators were behind us, but mid-level officials seemed to be protecting their turf. As the opening day of our school approached, I urged them to give us their attention, but they still didn't act. Finally, on the Friday before the Monday opening, I called six of the top officials in the city that supported our school, including the mayor and the head of the city building commission, and I explained the intransigence of the managers. I told them, "Students are arriving at our school on Monday, and you're going to have to come to our school to tell the parents that the city is closing our school. We've complied with every request well ahead of deadlines, but your middle managers have failed to give us the approvals we need to open the school. I have spent $120,000 of state funds to prepare the school to open, and I have contacted state attorneys about the problem. We are ready to pursue legal remedies because your managers have mismanaged our requests, and it will not be pleasant for your city. If you can't give me assurance that you will remedy the problem, our attorney will be there Monday morning."

Over the weekend, these officials used their power to get the managers unstuck. We opened at 8:00 on Monday morning, and by 10:00 o'clock, we had all the approvals we needed. Again, this story illustrates the importance of building relationships with key influencers in the community. Sooner or later, you'll need them to step in and use their power on your behalf.

Hire staff and faculty.

One of the most challenging, and yet inspiring, elements of preparing to open a school is the interview and hiring process for key staff and teachers. In the year before the state approves your petition, you have probably met with scores of teachers. When they grasp the vision for the school, the vast majority express interest in joining the faculty. Now that the charter has been approved, they ask for interviews. You may have numerous applicants for each position. The benefit of such wide interest is that you can choose the very best to teach children in your school, but telling the others the bad news is painful for them and for the school administrators.

> *One of the most challenging, and yet inspiring, elements of preparing to open a school is the interview and hiring process for key staff and teachers.*

In Texas, we are allowed to write at-will contracts for our teachers. I highly recommend this form of employment contract because it avoids any sense of entitlement. Since we've hired teachers who have proven their giftedness and passion for children, this form of contract isn't perceived as a threat to their employment in any way. They are focused on the vision to provide outstanding education and a supportive environment for the children in their classroom each day.

Obtain furnishings and books.

Those who plan to open a school find no shortage of educational suppliers who can provide desks, globes, tables, computers, lab equipment, and all the other furnishings required for a school. Their catalogs and showrooms contain a wide variety of attractive options to consider. In most cases, these vendors deliver within 10 weeks, but don't cut it too close. Our bank is pleased to loan funds for furnishings because state funding insures the charter's future income. Order well in advance to make sure there will be no problem with delivery and set up.

When I met local superintendents, I often asked them where they bought their furnishings and if they were pleased with them. These superintendents were more than happy to share this information with me, and their input often proved to be valuable as we made choices to furnish our classrooms and offices.

The state board of education provides free textbooks for each subject in each grade level. In most classes, six to eight options are available. The principal and assistant principal examine the books to see which ones fit their values and offer the best instruction for their students. Numerous (and often conflicting) reviews of every book are available to help school administrators make their selection decisions. In Texas, new titles are supposed to be offered every five years, but because of budgetary restraints, this cycle has been slowed considerably. As the charter school becomes established, the principal may chair a committee of people tasked with curricula assessment and book selection.

Most charter schools don't start with a full library, but state and federal grants are available to purchase books to build a reputable library. In addition, book fairs generate income to buy books for a library, and parent-teacher organizations can raise money for this purpose.

Enroll students.

The application for a charter required the founders to conduct meetings with parents to inform them about the school and indicate their intent to sign up their children for enrollment. Now the time has come to actually enroll these children in the school. State law requires open enrollment, so schools publicize the times and place where parents can come to enroll their children.

Certainly, not all the parents who indicated intent the previous year follow through by enrolling their children. Some have moved away, and some have changed their minds. For one reason or another, perhaps 15% to 20% of parents who sign up before the charter is approved don't follow through to actually enroll their children. Don't be surprised, and don't be alarmed. Society is a flowing river, and inevitably, situations change for some families. You might want to have a waiting list even before your charter is approved. If not, the state is probably convinced that if you got 1,000 signatures from parents to indicate their interest, you'll be able to find even more parents who grasp the purpose of the school and see enrollment in your school as a wonderful opportunity for their children.

To enroll their children in Life Schools, parents are required to produce eight documents:

- An original birth certificate,
- Academic records (if applicable),
- Files regarding behavior at the previous school (if applicable),
- Proof of immunizations,
- A one-page essay by each parent explaining why their child should be enrolled in Life School,
- A signed agreement for parents to attend monthly parenting seminars provided by Life School,
- An agreement that a parent or guardian will observe the child in the classroom at least once each semester, attend monthly private conferences with the teacher, and
- A signed statement that the parents or guardian has read the Life School Parent-Student Handbook and agree with our policies and system of discipline.

Establish the parent-teacher organization.

One of the core values of our school is parental involvement in teaching their children. In fact, we tell parents they are the primary teachers; we are simply there to help them impart life, wisdom, and knowledge to their kids. We expect parents to be actively involved in every aspect of their children's education. To give parents information and to help them find a unified voice, schools should sponsor a parent-teacher organization. The Life School organization is called "Parents as Partners," a name which avoids conflicts with the nation-wide PTA and PTO organizations. Each state and district has guidelines for these groups, but most founders and administrators already are very familiar with them.

BUNDLED ENTITLEMENTS

When we opened our first Life School, the state didn't provide start up funds. Today, however, things have changed. With the approved charter in hand, founders can apply for federal grants administered by the states. The state of Texas offers $200,000, Georgia offers $400,000, and some states offer pro rata funding on the proposed enrollment. These grants, of course, aren't guaranteed. I've known times when the state had the funds and a deadline to spend them. At that time, they were eager to write checks to fund new charter schools. But I've also experienced situations when the state funds seemed to dry up. If a newly approved school is denied grant money, the founders have to do what I did when federal funds weren't available — they have to find it anywhere they can in order to get ready to open their school. Today, however, charter schools aren't just an interesting, futuristic concept.

> *Hundreds of them are providing educational excellence throughout the country, so more individuals, businesses, and foundations see a new school as a worthy cause for their benevolent investments.*

Hundreds of them are providing educational excellence throughout the country, so more individuals, businesses, and foundations see a new school as a worthy cause for their benevolent investments.

One of the biggest reasons businesses fail is undercapitalization. Their founders don't have enough money to cover expenses during the start up period of the company's life. The same problem is all too common for charter schools. In many cases, founders are visionaries who care passionately about educating children, and they may not have business savvy. They assume they can get by with whatever money comes in, and they expect expenses to fit their budgetary projections. I strongly recommend that any organization, a business, a school, or a family, build contingency funds into their budget. I've seen unexpected things happen too many times. Sometimes expenses exceed anticipated projections, and sometimes income is delayed. Either way, an adequate contingency fund enables the founder and administrators to sleep at night. They've got enough to worry about without fretting about where additional money will come from so they can open the doors of the school.

The amount of money flowing in and out of a school budget is significant. Before the school opens, the founder or one of the key administrators can probably handle the income and expenses without much trouble. Someone with good financial sense needs to oversee the budget during this crucial period because money will be scarce. After the school opens, however, the state education agency usually requires that schools hire a Certified Pubic Accountant or a certified public school business manager. (Texas law requires an annual audit by a CPA.) Even if the top school officials have the ability to manage the funds, they need to devote their time to the students, parents, and teachers. Funds will be especially tight in the first two months the school is operating because in many states the report of attendance will be turned in well before funds are issued to cover the expenses incurred during that time. For that reason, schools need to plan on having enough funds available to cover two months of operations before the funds arrive.

THE POSSIBILITY OF USING CHURCH FACILITIES

In most churches, the facilities are only used about 25% of the time. Buildings and grounds are so expensive that it makes sense to explore ways to work with outside organizations to defray costs. Charter schools are a viable option to consider. Church leaders need to investigate the costs, primarily inconvenience, to the worshipping community, but they also should weigh the considerable benefits of having a school at their site. Several of our Life Schools use church facilities, and we've found it to work beautifully for both organizations.

To be sure, church members have to get used to their Sunday school classrooms having the look and feel of schoolrooms. In each room, two walls are filled with posters, graphs, portraits, and all the visual aids teachers need for their classes. The worship center is used for school assemblies. During the week, there may be competition for scheduling events, and in every part of the building the school uses, the facilities experience wear and tear. For symbiosis to work effectively, both parties have to be committed to excellent communication and flexibility.

The lease payments by the school can be 70% to 100% of the mortgage payments for the building, so the church benefits financially. Of course, as the lessee, the school can ask for particular building specifications from the church, the lessor, to accommodate the needs of the school. These specifications need to be clearly outlined in the preliminary conversations and lease negotiations to be sure new buildings or renovations comply with the school's requirements. In addition to building costs, when a school and a church share facilities, the school is expected to pay five-sevenths of the cost of utilities and maintenance. IRS guidelines, state educational agencies, and accepted accounting practice have determined that the church uses the facilities only a couple of nights a week and Sunday, so they are responsible for two-sevenths of these expenses.

Of course, church leaders often see beyond the obvious financial incentives to lease their facilities to charter schools. They care deeply about the people in the community, and they want to touch lives in every possible way. Many of these leaders have caught the vision for the life-changing blend of academic excellence and character development. They also realize that many of the families represented in the school don't currently attend any church in the community. The church certainly can't solicit parents or students to attend the church, but the connection is intuitively obvious. Parents and their children feel loved and supported at the school. Before the parents' eyes, children are growing, blossoming, and becoming strong, responsible, loving young adults, and they naturally gravitate to the church that sponsors the school. Studies show that 95% of Americans believe in God, but many haven't found a place to pursue God. It makes perfect sense that if they look for a faith community, the church that houses their charter school is an obvious place to look for a spiritual home.

> *Before the parents' eyes, children are growing, blossoming, and becoming strong, responsible, loving young adults, and they naturally gravitate to the church that sponsors the school.*

Why are churches willing to endure the additional building costs and inconvenience of housing a charter school? Certainly, the financial benefits are important, but far more, they know they are making a difference in the community by helping to provide quality education — and maybe, just maybe, they can earn the trust of parents and their children who may look to the church for spiritual guidance sometime in the future.

Today, a few visionaries in the realms of business and education believe a partnership between churches and charter schools is the most compelling hope for education in America. They have watched traditional public education decline across the nation in the past decades, and they realize change is necessary if our country is going to return to global leadership in science, technology, the arts, business, and politics. These entrepreneurs come from a conservative, faith-based view of life, and they see tremendous benefits in combining a faith foundation with academic excellence. Time will tell how their commitment to the future will shape the partnership between charter schools and churches, but I anticipate great things from them.

One of these visionary leaders who is already taking dramatic steps is David Green, the founder and president of Hobby Lobby. Mr. Green is putting his considerable resources to work to combine the causes of faith and education. In November of 2008, he gave a new church building on 10 acres, valued at $2.4 million, to The Oaks Fellowship, the church that leases space to one of our Life Schools and where my son, Scott, is the pastor. Soon, Scott and his pastoral team will open the church as an extension site for The Oaks Fellowship, and we'll begin a Life School in the building, too. Mr. Green believes in our vision to use thriving churches to house successful charter schools, and he is committed to provide properties for worthy churches and schools in urban areas around the country.

The benefits of charter schools leasing church facilities are very attractive to both parties, but let me offer a word of caution. Church leaders need to be very careful not to wink at the purpose of providing quality public education while they make plans to use the school as an evangelistic outreach. The integrity of the school must not be compromised in any way. It has a contract with the state to provide public education in the community. Though it may have Christian administrators and teachers, and though it may be housed in a church building, it isn't a Christian school. The spiritual impact of the school ultimately may be vast and deep, but it must be the spontaneous result of the credibility built by the school, not a primary purpose of the founders, administrators, or teachers.

WATCH FOR LAND MINES

Most people who know me would say that I'm a very diligent person who understands the value of the planning process as well as the importance of building strong relationships. The blend of those two elements — attention to details and establishing good will — is a formula for success in every area of life. I would have to say, however, that no matter how hard I've tried to be diligent and relational, every charter school I've opened has experienced significant difficulties with local city officials, the mid-level managers who can make things go smoothly or create frustrating bottlenecks. Perhaps I haven't worked hard enough to cast the vision for our school, but God knows I've tried!

> *The blend of those two elements — attention to details and establishing good will — is a formula for success in every area of life.*

After opening several schools and consulting with others who have opened schools, I have come to the conclusion that I need to anticipate this difficulty in every community. I need to do as much as possible to smooth the way, but I should never be surprised by roadblocks to permits and approvals thrown up by mid-level managers in city departments.

With this perspective, wisdom dictates that founders spend additional energy developing allies among top officials in each community. Then, when the time is right and intervention is necessary, these men and women can flex their muscles to get things moving.

In many ways, the months between the approval of the petition and the opening of the school's doors are some of the most exhilarating for an educator. The months and even years of dreaming about providing quality education for children is becoming a reality, but there's so much to do. Those who have worked through the laborious application process have proven they have the vision, tenacity, and love it takes to make the school a reality. These months will be incredibly busy, but they are tangible steps toward fulfillment of a dream.

June Rosdahl, Preston, and Mrs. Wilson

There is an old adage that says, "Two heads are better than one." This is clearly evident in the success story of a second grade student named Preston. Preston first came to me needing assistance in reading. I worked with him for nearly half a year in a small group setting before the wonderful transformation in his life — and that of his teachers.

His teacher, Mrs. Autumn Wilson, and I collaborated together from the very beginning as we attempted to unlock the reading difficulties and social complexities of this young boy. Our sense of urgency escalated as we noticed that Preston withdrew from most educational challenges. Our hearts sank as we often witnessed Preston close himself off from learning and normal interactions of a classroom. His coping mechanism would kick into high gear, and there was little either one of us could do to draw him out. His self-esteem was greatly impacted, and he often withdrew from his peers and his teachers.

Mrs. Wilson and I communicated frequently in an effort to help Preston. If a successful technique was achieved by one of us, it was shared with the other. When Preston faced a difficult day or an insurmountable impasse, we made sure the other knew of the difficulty. We looked after his best interests and were always looking for better solutions. Communication was the key, and it continued for several months. Together we found ways to encourage Preston and build his self-esteem. Slowly, we addressed areas of weaknesses in his reading, and evidence of progress began to show. He began to read with fluency and accuracy, and his evaluation scores soared. Most importantly, he stopped withdrawing from people and situations. Even from the beginning, the praise and encouragement never ceased. However, it began to escalate when we, including Preston, realized the tremendous gains he was making in reading. We were all astonished at his growth.

For Preston, academic growth and success was like a braid of interwoven threads. The braid began with the cooperation of his teacher and me, his reading coach, and it included the intertwining threads of other professional school personnel and family members. The building of peer relationships was entwined as well. As Preston's knowledge expanded, the threads began to strengthen.

The size of the threads and the braid itself became thicker as he matured as a reader and communicator. Preston developed a rich speaking vocabulary and excellent reading abilities. Now, he talks about his life and everyday experiences to reach out to those around him. Preston is so excited to be learning and reading! He uses reading to broaden his understanding of his world. Preston does not need my coaching assistance any longer. Together, Mrs. Wilson, other staff members, and I helped Preston become successful, which confirms that excellent education comes from many sources and angles. When we work together, the students win. Isn't that what it's all about?

In an effort to help Preston, Mrs. Wilson and I took extra time to talk with one another, but neither one of us realized just how crucial our communication would be. In it we found the small successes that would eventually lead to huge accomplishments in Preston's reading.

When purposeful intervention occurs in the lives of struggling students, they can make remarkable progress, and their lives are transformed. The lengthening and strengthening of the braid grows and cannot be easily broken. To do this, teachers must partner with other professionals and family members to create a bond so that student success is achieved to its fullest potential.

June Rosdahl
Reading Coach
Life School Red Oak

7 | THE SPIRIT OF THE CLASSROOM

Education is not the filling of a pail, but the lighting of a fire.
—William Butler Yeats, poet

The months and years of toil invested in preparatory analysis, drafting the charter, meeting with countless people, hiring staff, directing volunteers, and orchestrating all the details necessary to open the doors on the first day of school are well worth it because a charter school has the unspeakable opportunity to create a supportive, life-transforming culture in the classroom. The excited looks in children's eyes, the confidence of teachers, and the joy of parents at their children's success are wonderful rewards for our efforts. But an overwhelmingly positive classroom experience doesn't just happen. The charter sets the direction of the school by articulating the values that provide freedom for teachers to devote themselves wholeheartedly to their students each day. Paul L. Sadler, a member of the Texas State House of Representatives, observed that charter schools have a unique opportunity to create a new spirit in the classroom that equips students to excel for the rest of their lives. He said, "Educators would know a better way if they were free to do what they know to do. Charter schools could catch on to become the school system of the future. Charter schools could be the experimental ground for future schools. They could create a new kind of school meeting the special needs of children, and preparing students for the future."

A CULTURE OF LEARNING

A teacher has not taught until the pupil has learned, and the environment of the classroom determines a child's receptivity to instruction. A teacher may have written brilliant lesson plans, and she may be gifted and articulate in communicating the information, but if the systems don't allow her to control the atmosphere of the classroom, she won't be able to connect with the students to genuinely teach them. Teachers in public schools, especially in urban settings, feel that their hands are tied in their classes each day because they don't have control of students' behavior. Tragically, some of the students in these classes long to learn, but they are kept from learning because the teacher's attention is consumed by a few bad actors that disrupt the class. Far too often, teachers in public schools endure chaos instead of enjoying students' respect and cooperation. The values and systems articulated in a school charter, however, create the systems that can produce a culture of learning in which teachers delight in teaching and students revel in learning. For this reason, teachers who love to teach gravitate to excellent charter schools.

Over and over again, I've heard teachers who transferred to Life Schools tell me how much they love being at our schools. After they've been with us a couple of weeks to a month, they tell me that they've never felt so fulfilled. One teacher, whose comments represent dozens of others, explained that she had taught at the fifth-grade level in the three different public schools over the years. "At each school," she told me, "I was more of a policeman than a teacher. Some of the students disrupted class and made it virtually impossible for the rest of the children to learn. But here — oh my! — my classroom is a dream come true. Students are respectful and well behaved. They do their homework, they cooperate, and they are engaged in learning every single day." She sighed and told me, "Dr. Wilson, this is why I became a teacher. This is the way school ought to be."

CREATING THE CULTURE

Parents and their children who attend our charter schools are well informed about our expectations in the classroom. Before they walk through the door on their first day, they have read the Parents' Handbook, and they know that we put high value on respect, diligence, and excellence in everything that happens in the school. Because many public schools don't create this culture of learning, students react to the stress with either "fight or flight": their anger spills over into resentment toward authority and each other, or they withdraw emotionally and relationally from the perceived threats around them. Our task, and our high privilege, is to provide a safe place where students don't feel the urge to fight or flee. We want our classrooms to be havens of love and acceptance where students can feel relaxed so they can focus all their energies on learning and growing. To a remarkable extent, parents report that we are accomplishing our purpose.

> *We want our classrooms to be havens of love and acceptance where students can feel relaxed so they can focus all their energies on learning and growing.*

Our expectations of students are a reflection of the universal truths of honesty, integrity, and service found in the Ten Commandments, the Sermon on the Mount, and the apostle Paul's list of the "fruit of the Spirit." These expectations include five points:

Instant obedience.

Our concept of obedience isn't military precision that demands instantaneous compliance without question or reflection. Instead, it's appropriate response to appropriate authority. When the student doesn't understand a teacher's directions, an appropriate response is to ask the teacher to clarify or repeat the instruction. In many public schools, teachers aren't viewed as recognized authorities, so students don't feel they need to obey the teacher's instructions. Respect for properly constituted authority is central to order in the classroom.

Respect for others.

We are committed to cultural, racial, and economic inclusion. In other words, every person has intrinsic value and deserves respect. Instead of forming cliques that thrive on comparison and condemnation, we encourage peer mentoring so that students who are advanced in a subject can assist those who need additional help. This relationship sharpens the mentor and provides support for struggling students. In Life Schools, students as young as second, third, and fourth grades meet in peer groups to learn together and help one another. Fighting, of course, is out of bounds in every grade, and in fact, we teach our students that retaliation and self-defense are also wrong because they have another recourse: the recognized authority in the classroom is responsible to provide protection and can be trusted to defend those who are attacked. Similarly, abusive language isn't permitted in our schools. Cursing, name-calling, and demeaning language harm the hearer and demean the person speaking.

Respect for property.

Respecting property is simply an extension of students' respect for one another and themselves. When the culture of love and honor takes root in a school, theft and other destructive behaviors are minimized. When they occur, we require parents to pay for any damages or loss incurred by their child's behavior.

Diligence to duty.

Students in our schools make a commitment to do what they are assigned to do in the designated time with enthusiasm and as much excellence as they can muster. In each class, students work on their assignments to the best of their abilities. In physical education classes, every student is engaged in the activity. Some, of course, are more athletically gifted than others, but everyone participates and supports one another. Diligence, however, doesn't imply drudgery. In our schools, we look for any and every reason to celebrate, and we have a blast! We have parties for remarkable successes, holidays, and many other occasions. During these times, children are children. They laugh, shout, run, or whatever is appropriate at the time. We don't expect them to be quiet at a celebration. That wouldn't be appropriate. When we celebrate, we really enjoy ourselves, but the fun we have at parties never detracts from our academic pursuits. In fact, having fun together provides depth of experiences, richness in relationships, and a backdrop of delight for all of the hard work we require of our students. If a student is unresponsive and remains uninvolved, our policy is to intervene early to address the problem before it becomes an ingrained habit. At times, teachers have contacted parents about withdrawn students in the first weeks they attend our schools. When children fall behind, it's very difficult for them to catch up later. Early intervention often changes the direction of a student's career, and turns an insecure, uninvolved child into a glorious success story.

> *Early intervention often changes the direction of a student's career, and turns an insecure, uninvolved child into a glorious success story.*

Listening Learning Position.

We teach the Listening Learning Position (LLP) in kindergarten through elementary grades. The ritualized position for learning includes: hands in the lap, feet flat on the floor, eyes on the appropriate authority (most often the teacher), mouth closed, and ears open to hear. When the children assume the LLP, the nerve centers in the large muscles of the body "remember" and "remind" the brain that it's time to learn. Even in the upper grades, the spoken acronym "LLP" elicits an immediate response: the students take their seats, turn toward the appropriate authority, and focus attentively on the speaker.

When children fail to follow these clearly defined expectations, we implement "The Tally System," which is simply three pieces of paper that record (or tally) failure of a student to comply with these directives: one stays with the teacher, another is sent to the school office, and the student takes the other home to give to his or her parents. If there are three tallies in a week, the student serves a detention.

When we want to change students' behavior, we prefer the term "redirection" to "correction." Instead of saying, "Don't talk to me like that," we remind the student of his commitment: "You know you should respond with respect when an appropriate authority speaks to you," If a child is distracted, the teacher might say, "You should be giving attention to your class work now." And if a child is sitting alone and not participating in an activity, the teacher may say, "Come on and join us. We're all part of this activity, and we need you to help us." If the student responds to the teacher's admonition, there's usually no tally given at all. If, however, the student fails to respond, a tally is given. A student may have two tallies in a week without receiving a detention. For these tallies, the teacher calls the parents on the phone to report their child's behavior and discuss appropriate steps to remedy the problem. Typically, a teacher explains the situation to a parent and then asks for assistance: "You know your child much better than I do. Help me understand how to help him. I love your child, too, and I want to help him in any way I can. What's the key to reach your child?"

On Monday morning, all the previous week's tallies are erased and everyone starts over. If, however, a student is disciplined three times in a semester (each time represents three tallies in a week), a parent is required to come to the school to meet with an administrator before the student is allowed back in class. If a child receives a fourth discipline, he is suspended from school and must stay home for a day. Quite often, the suspension inconveniences the parent who works or had other plans, so now the parent is highly motivated to help the child change behavior. A fifth discipline necessitates a two-day suspension. A sixth discipline is very serious. One of our administrators calls the parents into the office to discuss the fact that only one more discipline means expulsion from our school, and if the student's behavior doesn't change, that's exactly what happens.

The process using The Tally System is clear and strong. It empowers the teacher to maintain discipline in the classroom, and it invites the student's parents to take action to correct their child's behavior. None of this is a surprise. No teacher can say she doesn't have control of her class. She does. And no parents can say they didn't know what would happen if their child misbehaves. The handbook was perfectly clear, and more importantly, the parents were told at every turn that they are their child's primary teachers.

In our schools, the culture we've created interrupts a student's slide toward anger and violence or toward fear and withdrawal. We've worked hard to build an atmosphere of respect and support for every student, and early intervention by teachers and parents nips most problems in the bud.

THE POWER OF PARENTS

The concerted actions by teachers and parents work wonders. In public schools, children often get away with behavior problems because they ignore their teacher's attempts at correction, and the parents aren't even aware of their child's discipline problems in the classroom. When teachers and parents are partners, the student receives attention — encouragement and consequences — both at school and at home, and change is reinforced by the two most important sources of authority in the child's life.

In the field of psychology, "triangles" in relationships are recognized as powerful and destructive. They form when two people take sides against the third, conveniently blaming the third party for any problems one of them might have. Blaming others effectively shifts and abdicates responsibility, preventing positive change. Teachers in public schools see triangles in action all too often. When a student has a behavior problem, the student tells his parents that it's the teacher's fault. Instead of pursuing truth, the parents too quickly jump to their child's defense (and more to the point, their own defense, because their child's misbehavior reflects negatively on them). The problem isn't solved, the teacher feels frustrated and helpless, and the child continues to develop a lifestyle of blame shifting, irresponsibility, and apathy toward authority.

Some of our teachers at Life Schools have told me that our emphasis on a strong partnership between parents and teachers has effectively stopped destructive triangles. One teacher remarked, "Dr. Wilson, thank you for how you've constructed this school. In the school where I used to teach, I often found that students blamed me for their poor behavior. The parents believed their child's story, and they were furious with me. When I went to the administration, they blamed me, too. I felt totally alone in my classroom, and the student sat there with a smile on his face because he thought he had won the game. I had ulcers from trying to sort out the truth and dodge the blame." Tears filled her eyes as she continued, "But here at our school, we're a team. I love the parents, and they love me. Together, we help their children become all they can be. The administration supports me, and the school administrators aren't afraid of being sued by parents. On top of all that, the students aren't caught in the middle of their teachers and their parents. When everyone is on the same team, everyone is at peace, and everyone succeeds. It's amazing!"

Children who think they've won in the parent-teacher-student blame game actually have lost in the most significant ways. They think they don't have to respect authority. Many of them who fail to respect authority in school never learn to respect any other authority, such as God and government's laws. Their unwillingness to follow leadership in the classroom may eventually lead to far greater consequences in society, such as jail, bankruptcy, and divorce. In our system, blaming parents or teachers isn't allowed. We seek truth, not blame. We want to redirect a child's behavior so that he learns to give and receive respect, not just manage his misbehavior to keep it at a minimum.

When children experience love and respect in the classroom, they develop that rare character quality in our culture: responsibility. As the children learn to embody these traits, they take them home with them every day, and they often have a dramatic impact on their parents and siblings. Parents not only notice the child's life is different; sometimes their child's example changes their lives, their marriages, and the atmosphere of the home. Siblings realize their brother or sister no longer is as self-absorbed, angry, and demanding. And in fact, he or she now treats others with respect and speaks the truth. In this way, the old saying, "a child will lead them," becomes a reality in these homes. It's a marvelous thing to see.

In the loving, strong, supportive atmosphere of Life Schools, we have experienced a very strange problem: students who are sick often beg their parents to take them to school anyway because they feel safe and loved at school. They often insist they aren't feeling bad. Later, when a teacher realizes the child is really ill, the office has to call the parent at home or at work to come pick up the child. It's an inconvenience, but it's also a wonderful statement about the atmosphere of love at our school.

PARENTS' SEMINARS

We believe very strongly that parents are the primary instructors of their children. Our teachers play a vital but secondary role. The spirit of the classroom is a reflection of our combined efforts to instill character, impart wisdom, and inspire children to academic success. At Life Schools, we don't just *hope* parents will be partners with our teachers — we *require* it, and we equip parents through seminars designed specifically for them. Each month, our teachers host meetings required for all parents, and after these meetings, we conduct seminars at each of our schools. In these topic-specific seminars, we have experts in the fields of parenting, marriage, and education to speak to our parents. At each campus, we offer three to five different topics, including "How to Help Your Child with Homework," "Family Finances," "How to Raise Your Children," "TAKS Tutoring," "Nutrition for Kids," and "Building a Strong, Loving Marriage." We invite noted authors and speakers to speak to our parents, and these experts are glad to speak at a public school. They often bring their books to sell to parents who want more information about the topic. Reading and applying the principles in these books deepens the impact of the speaker's message.

Parents are required by the school to attend the meeting with the teacher each month. They are required to participate in two parents' seminars each semester, but many find them so helpful that they attend each month. In our mobile society, many young parents live far from their own parents and extended family, and they often feel alone and inadequate in their parenting skills. They want help, and our seminars provide it. Some of them tell us that the lessons they learn at our seminars are revolutionary, and they have a dramatic impact on every aspect of their family's life. At this point, we'll have 3,500 to 4,000 parents in attendance at mandatory monthly meetings with teachers throughout our system, and about 2,000 attend the parents' seminars in a given month.

Because of tension between parents, teachers, and school administrators, many public schools don't emphasize parents meeting with teachers, and in some cases, they even discourage these interactions. Our philosophy and practice are quite the opposite. At every point, we encourage meaningful contacts between parents and their child's teacher. Quite often, teachers are on the sidewalk when parents drop off or pick up their kids. In these passing moments, a teacher might say, "Johnny's doing really well in math," or "Beth needs a bit more help in English. I'll call you later to talk about what we can do to help her." Whenever there's a problem, behavioral or academic, our teachers intervene early to contact parents to find a suitable remedy for the situation. No one blames, no one condemns, and no one needs to react defensively. From the first day, parents and teachers understand that they are partners, not adversaries. For children to receive the best education and develop qualities of character, parents and teachers must see each other as allies.

When parents and teachers are partners in educating children, everybody wins. Parents stop blaming teachers for their child's problems that actually originate from their own shortcomings, teachers don't feel isolated and impotent in dealing with children, and children soon realize they can no longer play teachers and parents against each other. The dance of manipulation and blame stops, and genuine progress takes place in equipping the child and the parents for a productive future. When people live in triangles of blame, they can avoid the real issues of hurt, anger, and irresponsible behavior. But when each person is committed to truth, respect, and responsibility, each one learns to live in authenticity and integrity. Instead of arguing or avoiding each other most of the time, family members find common purpose in developing character qualities and pursuing worthwhile goals. Does this seem like a dream? Can it really happen in a public school? Yes, I assure you it can. I've seen it countless times with my own eyes.[15]

We give all the parents of our students a list of the character qualities we want to instill in their children's lives, and the list includes a brief description of each one. (See the list in the appendix.) They don't have to wonder what Life Schools are about. If they want, we can have the list laminated so they can carry it around in their pockets to remind them of our shared priority to equip their children, not only with knowledge, but also with transformative life skills. School administrators in Texas have noticed the impact of creating a partnership between parents and teachers to impart character to students at Life Schools. The Texas Education Agency has adopted our emphasis on character development, and they make the curriculum available to any school in the state. Principals

---

15 For more on destructive triangles in relationships, see *The Dance of Anger* by Harriett Goldhor Lerner, Chapters 8 and 9.

and superintendents who grasp the importance of character development are using our material to change the lives of their students. I'm very grateful for their interest in our work.

ALWAYS EQUIPPING

We are deeply invested in equipping our teachers to relate effectively to students and parents. To reinforce our purpose and equip our staff, principals in our schools meet with teachers and administrators every Tuesday afternoon for an hour. Before school starts each August, we host a weeklong in-service training for our staff, and we invite some of the finest speakers in education to train our people. This week refreshes our staff before the year begins, reminding all of us of our purpose, and building our sense of being a team. It's an exciting week, and it prepares us for a wonderful year together. During the year, we host daylong seminars for our staff on four separate days when school isn't in session. These days are "booster shots" to renew our vision and enthusiasm for our work with students and parents.

> *These days are "booster shots" to renew our vision and enthusiasm for our work with students and parents.*

In addition, we provide opportunities on campus twice a week after school for our staff to pursue a master's degree in counseling or school administration from one of two noted universities in our area. To help them pay for their courses, the universities offer a partial scholarship of one-third of the fees, and Life School pays for one-third of their expenses. Our administrators and teachers pay the other third of the cost of their course work. They can have their degrees in only three years, while they continue to teach and work in administration at our schools.

The spirit of the classroom is never an accident. In many public schools, disrespect and apathy are the result of over-regulation and a lack of emphasis on character development. In Life Schools, we have the distinct privilege of crafting a culture of love and responsibility so that every student, every parent, every teacher, and every administrator feels inspired to excel every single day.

Ellen Miller

When you walk into the doors of Life School and see teachers and children smiling, you realize there is something very special and different about this school. That's what happened to me the first time I ventured in to check out Life School Red Oak. We are now in our fourth year at LSRO, and I am still so grateful to have learned about this school and that there really is something very special and different about it.

I was particularly worried about our oldest child while he was attending public school. He was unhappy and was not performing academically to his potential. He dreaded going to school every day. I felt helpless as I saw him "slipping through the cracks." Then I heard about Life School Red Oak through a friend and went there to investigate its possibilities. I was impressed as I walked down the halls and looked inside the classrooms. The doors were open, but it was quiet! The students looked happy as they carried on with their activities. The teachers looked happy as well and obviously had control of their classrooms. I thought to myself, "This is the school for our children!" When we transferred our three children from public school to LSRO, we saw an immediate and positive change in their attitudes toward school, achievement, and academic progress. We saw a complete turn-around with our oldest child. He was happy! He was learning! He was making good grades! He was having no problems. What more could we ask?

All three children are happy, love their school, perform well academically, and I attribute that to the loving, caring attitude of the teachers and administration. The teachers truly care about and get to know each child, so there is more of a personal relationship between teachers and students than often occurs in public school classrooms. Also, since Life School is based on building character, I feel our children will become better citizens and well prepared for college. We are forever grateful to Life School!

Ellen Miller
Teacher's Aide, Life School Red Oak

Taking Texas State Senator Florence Sharpiro around Life School

8 | Steps You Can Take

If a child is to keep alive his inborn sense of wonder, he needs the companionship of at least one adult who can share it, rediscovering with him the joy, excitement and mystery of the world we live in.
—Rachel Carson, author

Vision, wisdom, and boldness. If you've read this far in this book, you have a heart for children to receive an education that equips them academically and develops their character. You may be a professional educator, or you may be a concerned parent or a community leader. If you are considering establishing a charter school, you need a clear vision, the depths of wisdom to know how to proceed, and boldness to open doors you may not have known even existed before you started the application process. In this chapter, I want to address the steps individuals can take to make the dream of a charter school a reality.

The steps I suggest aren't just abstract, untried concepts. Every year, the charter school movement is strong and is growing even stronger. For the past 20 years, across the administrations of four United States presidents, the Department of Education and the Congress have worked with 40 states to provide legislation and funds for the creation of charter schools. They are much more than a good idea; charter schools are a successful reality in American education today.

IF YOU ARE A FOUNDER

Founders combine two crucial traits: they care passionately about creating a different environment or culture, and they possess an entrepreneur's courage to find a solution no matter what obstacles they face. They simply aren't willing to take "No" for an answer. Like it was yesterday, I vividly recall the day those two factors came together in my life. I had been involved in Christian education for many years, but our school didn't have the resources or the power to change the culture. As I saw the emptiness in the lives of young people coupled with the devastation of drugs and violence, my heart broke. Young people I loved were ruining their own lives and killing one another. Something had to be done!

In the New Testament, Matthew tells us that Jesus had a moment like this. He records, "When [Jesus] saw the crowds, he had compassion on them, because they were harassed and helpless, like sheep without a shepherd" (Matthew 9:36). Their most basic needs, Jesus noticed, weren't being met by society. His solution was twofold. First, he marshaled the resources of caring people to reach out and care for these needy people, and second, he gave everything he had, including his own life, to solve their most pressing problem.

At that moment, I was willing to do absolutely anything to change the lives of these young people. I realized that the problem wasn't just that a few students were making horrible decisions. The underlying problem was that their culture was full of darkness, hopelessness, and despair. All day every day, they felt "harassed and helpless, like sheep without a shepherd." Changing their culture would take radical action, not just uttering some platitudes. God gave me a vision to touch their lives when they were young, to instill character and hope so that the trajectory of their lives would be positive instead of negative. It took a bit of time for the vision to coalesce and take shape, but

> *Changing their culture would take radical action, not just uttering some platitudes.*

the passion to change young lives was the genesis of our charter schools.

Our design is to change the worldview of students. We don't just talk about great music; we take them to the finest concert halls in the city to listen to the symphony and feel the power and beauty of their music. We don't just talk about outstanding works of literature; we visit the most outstanding libraries in our area to put great books in students' hands. We impart the skills of intentional decision making so they can make good choices no matter what temptations they face. They don't have to do what "everybody else" is doing. Instead, with a clear sense of purpose for their lives, they can choose a path that navigates around dangers and gets them where they want to go. We teach our students to face reality and grow stronger instead of escaping negative realities by medicating painful feelings.

If you are gripped by the needs of young people and you're willing to pay the price to step into their lives to be a charter school founder, I have a few suggestions for you. Immerse yourself in the realities of the youth culture. In most cases, you won't have to look very hard to have your heart broken. I know of school districts that can't find enough teachers, so classrooms have too many children or districts hire untrained teachers to fill positions. In a district near us, only 29% of the students graduate. The statistics and newspaper articles, however, tell only part of the story. Even for young men and women who graduate and those who aren't involved in violent activities, many live in a school world dominated by tension, fear, and anger. Their goal isn't to thrive and focus on the future, but to survive one more day so they can eventually graduate.

If you want to be the founder, CEO, or headmaster of a new charter school, enflame your passion by spending time around like-minded people. Conversations and insights about changing the culture for students will keep your vision fresh and strong. Also, explore several models of charter schools to see which one is the best pattern for the school you want to establish. Examine the systems, policies, procedures, and legal documents, and make sure to study your state's requirements. You will probably find that you resonate with the educators and systems of some charter schools more than others. Be an excellent student of existing charter schools. If you don't find ones you like in your area, travel to find ones that can serve as a template for the school you want to establish.

Crafting a clear vision is your first and primary task as a founder. Founding a charter school may begin with a vague sense of need. Sooner or later, this sense of need becomes a dream of a way to meet the need, but a dream isn't enough. It has to take shape and become a clear, compelling vision that can be translated into detailed strategies, systems, and timetables.

There are, I assure you, much easier ways to spend your time and energies. Being a founder of a charter school isn't a picnic in the park. It requires tenacity — a rare character quality, especially in our culture today. There will be oceans of paperwork to wade through, a myriad of questions to answer, and opposition where you least expected it. If prospective founders aren't gripped by the crushing need of young people, they'll be tempted to quit along the way, but if the faces of hurting children are burned into their consciences, these founders won't let anything stop them from creating a safe, positive, stimulating environment that genuinely changes lives.

IF YOU ARE A PRINCIPAL

I've talked to many gifted public school principals who feel supremely frustrated because they spend so much of their time managing mediocrity and trying to control the damage caused by bad actors in their classrooms. They try their best each day, but parents and teachers blame them for every conceivable problem. Excessive regulations of the state and the district feel like a straightjacket that prevents them from implementing needed changes. Some of these regulations were designed to control the behavior of the most incorrigible students in the school, but these regulations had the unintended consequence of suppressing excellence in the classroom. Too much bureaucracy inevitably produces mediocrity. Principals in traditional public schools do their best, but quite often, they only "muddle through" each day.

These professionals got into education because they wanted to make a profound difference in young people's lives, but many of them don't believe they are making more than a dent. Much of the literature reinforces this sense of despair. Some of the sharpest minds in the field of education recognize the bleak realities of the system and, after describing the benefits and shortcomings of various philosophies of education, they recommend that professional educators embrace the limitations of the existing systems and settle for getting by each day. The principals I've talked with want more — much more — than just getting by. They long to create or find a school environment they can pour their hearts into each day. Charter schools may be an answer for them.

> *These professionals got into education because they wanted to make a profound difference in young people's lives, but many of them don't believe they are making more than a dent.*

If you are a public school principal and the message of this book has awakened your desire to create a strong, positive culture in a school, you can do much more than manage chaos each day. You can construct a school environment that builds character on a foundation of trust and respect. You can orchestrate a system that attracts and supports the finest teachers in your community. In short, your dreams can become a reality.

My advice to you, dear principal, is the inscription on the Temple of Apollo at Delphi in ancient Greece: "Know thyself." Understand your strengths and limitations, and chart your course accordingly. Obviously, if you are a principal, you have administrative abilities, and you may also possess the skills of an entrepreneur as a founder of a charter school. That role requires boldness and courage in large measures. If you don't have a founder's profile, consider enlisting a founder to work with you. You can provide valuable support and insight as this person tenaciously wades through the application process. Or perhaps, you may put together a consortium of gifted people to work together to start a school in your community. And finally, another option is to find an existing charter school that is expanding, or a new school that needs a principal, and apply for the position.

No matter which direction you choose, don't let your passion for quality education wither away. You may be tired of the struggle and discouraged that your hopes haven't been fulfilled, but don't give up. Talk to principals of charter schools, and let their experiences fill your heart and rekindle your hope.

IF YOU ARE A TEACHER

Quite often, teachers feel more hopeless and helpless than their principals because they wield less power. When these wonderful men and women were training in college to become teachers, they dreamed of welcoming students into their well-ordered classroom, inspiring them to excellence, reinforcing qualities of character — and enjoying every minute of it. But for most of them, the reality of the classroom has proven to be far different than what they imagined. At first, disappointments weren't devastating because there was still hope for change. But gradually, the oppressive system of regulations drained most of the hope from their hearts, and they learned to settle for morsels falling from the table of public education. Charter schools, though, are a fresh source of inspiration and hope.

If there are charter schools in your area, visit them, talk to the teachers, and if it looks promising, schedule an interview with the principal. If your community doesn't have a charter school, look for a founder (and perhaps, other educational professionals) considering this option, and get in on the ground floor of the new venture.

When I started the Life School in Oak Cliff, two dedicated teachers worked with me hand-in-glove as we created all the systems and completed the petitioning process with the state. I don't know what I would have done without them. We formed a team, and together, we created a new culture for students.

In the last several years, a few people have asked me if teachers can become founders of charter schools. My answer is, "Of course they can," but it's the exception rather than the rule. The personality profile of the vast majority of teachers, coupled with their training and experience, makes them highly qualified to impart truth, skills, and character to young lives. They are not, as a group, inclined toward entrepreneurial pursuits. If they had those strengths, they would have gone into business, not education. Occasionally, though, I find a teacher with a unique set of gifts and experiences that equip him or her to be a charter school founder.

> *In the last several years, a few people have asked me if teachers can become founders of charter schools.*

As I've written earlier in this book, I believe that teachers are the lifeblood of any school. Every school needs to attract the finest and brightest teachers, and then it needs to free them to do what their training has equipped them to do. But training is only part of the equation of great teaching; the other part — an even bigger part, in my estimation — is for schools to continue to enflame the desires of every teacher to make a difference in the lives of their students. Excellent administrators don't encumber their teachers with excessive rules and regulations. Instead, they create an environment of respect and responsibility where excellence can thrive each day. In this kind of environment, teachers give everything they've got all day every day. They love coming to school each day, and the students love learning. I know. I've seen it in their eyes day after day at our schools.

IF YOU ARE A PARENT

Most parents aren't even aware that charter schools can make a profound difference in the education of their children, but when they find out, many of them eagerly pursue more information about these schools. In Texas, and probably in most other states, parents can go online to the state education agency's web site to find existing charter schools in their area. If there's not a charter school nearby, parents have several options. If a parent has the passion and entrepreneurial gifts required, he or she can become a founder, or a group of concerned parents may ask someone else to take this crucial role.

Parents can play an important part in the start up process. Some may assume the responsibility of signing up hundreds of other parents to enroll their children, and some may volunteer to help in other ways during different phases of exploration, petition, and preparation for the school to begin operations. As I've mentioned earlier in the book, I believe that parents are the primary educators of their children (for a biblical point of view about the role of parents teaching their children, see Deuteronomy 6). Teachers in public schools can certainly assist parents, but too often, parents and teachers keep their distance from one another instead of forming a powerful team. Charter schools, however, may provide the very best support a parent can get in this effort.

Many people think charter schools are good options in cities where public education struggles under the weight of poverty, broken families, drugs, and violence, but suburban areas are viable candidates for charter schools, too. In the suburbs, the problems aren't financial; they're spiritual. Affluence and conspicuous consumption steal the hearts of young and old. Students focus on possessions, and many of them waste their abilities and mortgage their futures for short-term pleasures. Parents in the suburbs, then, can be just as brokenhearted about their children as their neighbors downtown.

In an affluent suburb of Dallas, a large group of parents became dissatisfied with the amoral culture in public schools. They banded together, formed an organization, and researched the possibility of starting a charter school. When they began, they didn't have any professional educators involved, but their commitment to their children kept their vision strong during the long process of finding a consultant, drafting their petition, and doing all the preparatory work to start their school.

Parents don't need professional degrees in education to start a charter school. They just have to care enough, knock on enough doors, and keep mustering the courage to make their dream come true. Today, only 2% of students in America attend charter schools, but federal and state education agencies are making enormous amounts of resources available to start more of them. Parents with vision — in the cities, the suburbs, or in rural areas — don't have to stand by and watch their children endure inferior education in a fear-inducing environment. They can take action to change their children's world.

> *Parents don't need professional degrees in education to start a charter school. They just have to care enough, knock on enough doors, and keep mustering the courage to make their dream come true.*

IF YOU ARE A PASTOR

As a pastor, I have the greatest esteem and the highest hopes for those who serve God faithfully every day. People come to them to share their deepest needs, and these compassionate ministers give every ounce of heart and skill to bring healing to broken people. I believe charter schools offer a phenomenal opportunity for pastors to touch lives in their communities, but they need to be very careful to examine their motives. I've talked with some whose churches sponsored private Christian schools. When these schools struggled financially, some of these pastors began to see charter schools as a door to new resources. They intended to use public funds and mask the Christian emphasis in education at their school. This purpose is a breach of the state-charter school contract, and it must be avoided at all costs.

Pastors who are considering the possibility of hosting a charter school on their campus must keep two purposes completely separate. First, they must be committed to educational excellence according to the state guidelines. And second, they cannot and must not use the school to clandestinely teach Christian doctrine. They may, as my own experience can attest, face considerable opposition from good-hearted parishioners who don't understand this dichotomy and insist that the charter school be a source of Christian education. The first task of these pastors, then, is to educate their own people about the purpose and content of the charter school.

I believe that hosting a first-class charter school committed to the finest in public education gives the church a platform in the community like nothing else it can do. When the apostle Paul went to Athens, he walked through the Agora, the public market, and up Mars Hill, the seat of local government. There, he related to everyone who would listen. Today, too many churches stay in their "holy huddle," isolated from meaningful involvement in the community, and branded "irrelevant" by people in the marketplace and in government. The process of applying for a charter puts founders in contact with every element of the local community. To get state approval, they have to make meaningful contact with people in every area of society: government, business, and education. And after the school is open and parents and children experience a supportive, warm, loving, powerfully transformative environment, many of them naturally connect the dots between the school and the church. When that occurs, the church doesn't have to promote itself, and it doesn't have to look over its shoulder

> *I believe that hosting a first-class charter school committed to the finest in public education gives the church a platform in the community like nothing else it can do.*

to make sure the state doesn't catch them proselytizing. Providing quality public education is its goal each day. An attractive reputation in the community is simply a natural byproduct and benefit.

Another reason a church may consider hosting a charter school is the financial benefit. To make their existing facilities suitable for a charter school, most churches will need to invest in significant renovation. This investment, however, can prove to be monetarily rewarding. I know of relationships in which the charter school's lease pays 100% of the church's mortgage each month, and others where the lease pays 70% of the mortgage. In addition, the standard operating procedure (SOP) of CPAs (developed primarily for parochial accounting) allows the school to pay for five-sevenths of the utilities and upkeep of leased church (non-profit) facilities. This financial arrangement is very attractive to many churches, but again, pastors and other church leaders need to evaluate their motives to be sure their interest in charter schools is noble and right.

The profile of successful pastors varies widely. Some are gifted teachers, and they devote most of their time in message preparation and delivery. Many are compassionate shepherds who delight in caring for the hurting and giving direction to those who wander. A few have administrative strengths and direct those under them to be effective, and a few have the abilities of a CEO, full of vision and energy to accomplish great things. Most pastors aren't entrepreneurs and won't assume the role of founder for a charter school. Even those who are entrepreneurial by nature need to find a layperson in the community to spearhead the effort because their title as pastor often makes them suspect to the state education agency. The officials at the state office are suspicious of anyone who might attempt a syncretism of public education with Christian influences, so it's best for a visionary pastor to play a support role in the founding of a charter school.

People may look at me and say, "Tom, you're a pastor. Why do you give advice like this?"

My answer is that I stepped out of the role of pastor before we petitioned the state. At that point, I was a professional educator, not a pastor. My experience as a pastor and Christian school educator taught me many valuable lessons, but I knew I had to focus my energies on public education to accomplish my goal of starting a charter school.

I believe the American church is on the verge of being marginalized in our culture. Many studies show that people increasingly see the church and its message as "nice" but "not necessary" and "not relevant" to their lives. In an attempt to become relevant, too many church leaders have adapted their message to suit people who come to their churches, but with disastrous results. In his recent book, *The Great Omission,* Dallas Willard described the way churches are drifting along with the consumer-mentality of our culture. In an interview on this topic, Willard observed, "We are designed to be creators, initiators, not just receivers. Yet the whole model, the consumerist model of the human being, is to make us passive, and to make us complainers and whiners, because we're not being given what we need. We cook up a 'right' to that and then we say we've been deprived of our rights. We see this in our churches, which pander to consumers. They say, 'Come and consume the services we offer, and we guarantee you a wonderful time. You'll go out of the church door feeling good.' "[16] But feeling good isn't God's goal for the church. He wants believers to be strong, vibrant models of grace and truth in every arena of life, including public education. We can't become those models if we're only trying to "fit in."

Some say that we now live in a post-Christian era, but I think that age has passed. Today, we live in a pre-Christian age much like the first century when Paul carried the message of Christ to people who held a wide variety of beliefs about God and the meaning of life. Secularists in government, media, and education give

---

16 Cited by Luci Shaw in an interview with Dallas Willard, "Spiritual Disciplines in a Postmodern World," *Radix* magazine, Vol. 27, No. 2.]

passing lip service to spirituality, but their unbelieving philosophies increasingly dominate every aspect of our culture. "Christian America" of 50 years ago no longer exists. We are mistaken (and foolish) if we continue to think that most people truly believe in God and are loyal to the church. Yes, the vast majority of people still profess to have some religious faith, but if you scratch below the surface and ask about the content of their faith, the answers are alarmingly shallow. David Kinnaman, director of a Barna study of spirituality in America, reflects, "In fact, one reason why beliefs fluctuate is that most Americans hold few convictions about their faith. For instance, even among those who disagree with orthodox views, many do so while hedging their bets. Most Americans have one foot in the biblical camp, and one foot outside it. They say they are committed, but to what? They are spiritually active, but to what end? The spiritual profile of American Christianity is not unlike a lukewarm church that the Bible warns about."[17]

If the church doesn't do something to prove itself to the community, it will become even more irrelevant and continue to slide into obsolescence. Charter schools offer a source of light in the darkness. Quality public education, imparted by the finest teachers in an atmosphere of love and respect, demonstrates the value of character in today's world. If churches are the lighthouses for these shining beacons, people will look to the church for more than excellence in education. But make no mistake. The process of applying for a charter requires incredible tenacity and diplomacy, and the concerted efforts of a dedicated team of people. The benefits are attractive, but the price must be paid to achieve the desired results. No shortcuts will work — only hard work fueled by compassion for children and a passion to equip them for the future.

---

17 "Barna's Annual Tracking Study Shows Americans Stay Spiritually Active, But Biblical Views Wane," www.barna.org/FlexPage.aspx?Page=BarnaUpdateNarrowPreview&BarnaUpdateID=271.

IF YOU ARE A DONOR

I know a number of wealthy people who care deeply about the plight of public education in America, and they want to invest their resources to right the ship. These men and women feel enormously blessed by the values and economic opportunities in our country, and it breaks their hearts to see the American way of life deteriorate. They believe the decline of education, in academics in the cities and in the moral climate in the suburbs, must be reversed if America is going to reestablish its place of greatness. These people built successful, prosperous systems, and they have devoted considerable amounts of their wealth and their energies to change the face of public education.

Though the states fund the daily operations of charter schools, most states don't provide funding for facilities. Many of these wealthy people are entrepreneurs looking for charter school founders as partners. In a few cases, these donors have given millions to churches, but they've been disappointed by the way the funds have been used. Now they want to invest in a more innovative solution: a partnership between churches and charter schools. Some are willing to buy buildings and give them to churches that will host a charter school at the site. A few times, however, gifts of buildings had a surprisingly negative impact. The church didn't have the money for renovation so the building remained empty for a long time. Some shrewd investors observed this problem and made commitments to fund the renovation of those buildings to make them suitable for both purposes: the church and the charter school. I've also talked to donors who want to fund the start up costs during the application process and the months of preparation before the school doors open.

Of course, most of the people who have made fortunes in business have also made friends in high places in government, so their influence can go beyond writing checks for charter schools.

Of course, most of the people who have made fortunes in business have also made friends in high places in government, so their influence can go beyond writing checks for charter schools. Quite often, they have close relationships (or at least, excellent reputations) with key legislators and officials in state and federal offices. A phone call from them can be very persuasive, and at times, determinative when founders face roadblocks in the application process.

OVERCOMING INERTIA

When Franklin Roosevelt faced the depths of the Depression in the First 100 Days of his administration, the country was in dire straights. Hundreds of banks had failed, and millions of people had lost their jobs. At that crucial moment in our nation's history, many people wondered if democracy was still a viable option. Some believed communism would be a better solution, but others leaned right toward fascism. Roosevelt instinctively sensed that the American people desperately needed hope coupled with tangible steps of progress. In his first inaugural address, he famously changed the tenor of the nation when he told people, "The only thing we have to fear is fear itself." And from that day forward, Roosevelt sent a raft of bills to Congress to get America working again. Inactivity, he knew, would cripple the country emotionally and economically, and he wasn't concerned if a particular bill in the New Deal proved ineffective. "Try something," he told his staff. "If it doesn't work, try something else."

Today, we face a crisis of confidence in American education. In countless classrooms in our country, teachers feel a crushing oppression of well meaning but excessive regulations that have a negative impact on the classroom. Instead of fostering respect and excellence, teachers spend an inordinate amount of time and precious energy managing misbehavior of a few students, inadvertently neglecting the opportunities of others. This drift has occurred for decades, but it can be reversed. Like Roosevelt, leaders today can inject a fresh sense of hope in public education and take bold action to create much needed change. Basic physics tells us that overcoming initial inertia requires more force than keeping a body in motion, so leaders need to recognize the extra effort needed to begin the process of change. Ingrained habits die hard, and people in authority have a vested interest in maintaining the status quo, but vision, passion, and tenacity can work wonders.

Painter Henri Matisse remarked, "To look at something as though we had never seen it before requires great courage." No matter who you are and what your title may be, you can play a vital role in changing the shape of public education in your community. You may have entrepreneurial strengths, and you can gather a team around you. Or perhaps you work more effectively as a valued member of the team. Whatever your role may be, don't let fear and difficulty prevent your vision for your children from becoming a reality. Be strong, be creative, be courageous — and don't take "No" for an answer.

Scott Wilson

As a pastor, my calling is to touch the lives of people in our community with the love of God. There are many ways to accomplish this purpose, but from my perspective, one of the most effective is partnering with a charter school. In fact our strategy to start new, thriving churches is built around this partnership.

When my Dad started the Life School in Oak Cliff years ago, I was excited, but I didn't realize it would have such a profound impact on the church and the community. As I watched the school get off the ground, I caught his vision for providing quality education for disadvantaged students. Many of the students who came to the school were, to be frank, underperforming. But before my eyes, Life School changed lives. Outbursts of anger and rebellion, which had been everyday experiences at their previous schools, gradually were replaced with harmony and a sense of purpose. These kids began to really learn, and even more important, their characters changed. As children's lives were transformed, their parents sat up and noticed. Countless parents told us they were amazed at the change in their children's lives. Their appreciation provided an open door for our church. The school's academic excellence and commitment to build character gave the partnering church credibility, and hundreds of parents started attending our church.

The relationship worked so well that we've started other churches and schools simultaneously. When we opened a school in one community, only 18% of the students passed the state test. By the end of the first year, an amazing thing happened: 82% passed. That's credibility!

Jesus told his followers not only to share the message of the gospel, but also to back up the message by serving people who desperately need help. He said to care for people who are hungry, thirsty, lonely, naked, sick, and prisoners. Today in America, he would point to inner city kids and wayward, affluent children in the suburbs, and he'd say, "See them. They're suffering, and they need your help. What are you doing to care for them?"

There are countless good programs we could use to help people in our communities, and lots of strategies to reach out to people who aren't yet part of the family of God. Partnering with charter schools, though, has proven to be incredibly powerful. By letting outstanding schools meet in our facilities, we tell the community that we care about them, we love their children, and we are here to help them in every way we can. Over the past 10 years, we've seen broken families mended, wayward and hopeless children gain a new sense of purpose, and overwhelmed parents now active in their children's development. And we've seen hundreds of people who didn't have a spiritual home find one in the churches where their kids go to school.

I hope other pastors will consider partnering with charter schools. It takes some coordination, but every program requires some effort. But I can't imagine a bigger return for the time and energy we've invested in our relationship with charter schools.

Scott Wilson
Pastor, The Oaks Fellowship

9 | My Legacy, Your Legacy

*Unless commitment is made, there are only promises and hopes
. . . but no plans.*
—*Peter Drucker, author and management consultant*

I believe every person has an innate, God-given desire to make a difference in the lives of others. In a similar vein, William James wrote, "The greatest use of a life is to spend it for something that outlasts it." My work to create charter schools is, to a significant degree, the historical legacy passed down to me from my grandfather and my father, and now, three of my sons are involved in education, too. I'm thrilled to be a part of a vision much larger than myself, but I know I'm not alone. Every person reading this book has the same longing and hope.

A LOOK AT THE SCRAPBOOK

My grandfather, Elijah Wilson, was born in 1865 in Joshua, Texas. He became a teacher, and in those days, a teacher taught all subjects in all grades. By 1890, he became the headmaster of a larger school in Midlothian, Texas, which met at the St. Paul Methodist Church two miles from the town. Shortly after he assumed the role, the pastor of the church died. The leaders of the church respected my grandfather, and they asked him to become the pastor of the church. In that community, he continued the dual roles of headmaster and pastor until he died in 1916.[18]

My grandfather had eleven children. His second wife, Maude, was my paternal grandmother. She was still a young woman when he died. By that time, she had borne four children. Like my grandfather, she had received an advanced education. She taught music and wrote poetry and prose. At the school, she taught elocution, the ability to speak or read aloud in public.

> *Like my grandfather, she had received an advanced education. She taught music and wrote poetry and prose. At the school, she taught elocution, the ability to speak or read aloud in public.*

My dad, Vernon Edgar Wilson, was eight years old when his father died. When Dad was twelve, times were very hard in central Texas. My grandmother's income was severely limited, and she had trouble making enough money to feed and clothe the children. She wrote plays, poetry, and sayings, and she traveled to schools in neighboring communities to speak at local gatherings. At these events, she taught elocution by having students recite poetry or read a passage to the gathering. She had written about 30 small books, and she supplemented her income by selling those at the performances of elocution. In hard times, many people couldn't afford the luxury of paying for entertainment, so her resources dried up. Her meager resources would have to be spent on her daughters. She told my father he would have to leave and make it on his own.

When my father left home, he got a ride north to Dallas. For the first few months, he lived under bridges and eked out a living selling newspapers. In the days before cell phones and email, communications were far more primitive, but after a while, one of his

---

18 Ironically, the church I pastored and the school I now lead is less than twenty miles from the location of my grandfather's church and school.

half-sisters, Abigail Fowler, heard about his predicament, and she invited him to live with her in Dallas. My dad lived with Abigail for several years, and during this time, he attended a Baptist church with her and her family.

After a couple of years, my father moved to Waxahachie in central Texas, where he attended high school. There, he and Paul Richards became star athletes and were standouts on the 1927 Texas high school state championship baseball team. After graduation, Dad played semi-professional baseball with Paul Richards, both of whom were proficient home run hitters. Later in his career, Richards would go on to far greater fame in the major leagues. My father's baseball career was cut short by a knee injury, but he enjoyed wonderful memories of those days playing ball.

After his aborted baseball career, Dad opened a trucking business hauling gravel in Dallas. He was an entrepreneur, so having only one business venture wasn't enough for him. He opened a restaurant across from Southern Methodist University called Shorty's Waffle House. To generate more income, he put nickelodeons in restaurants, dance halls, and other public places. All of these endeavors proved to be thriving businesses.

God, though, had other plans for my father. At the height of his success, Dad became a committed Christian, and he sensed God calling him to full-time ministry as a pastor. Dad never did anything halfway, so he sold all his businesses so he could devote himself wholeheartedly to the ministry. He went to seminary to be trained, and after graduation, he became a church pastor.

Not surprisingly, Dad valued hard work and self-reliance, and he imparted those values to his children. Without a trace of self-pity or bitterness, he told us stories of his childhood when he lived under a bridge and how

> *Without a trace of self-pity or bitterness, he told us stories of his childhood when he lived under a bridge and how he had earned nickels and dimes to pay for food.*

he had earned nickels and dimes to pay for food. I vividly recall that when my brother and I asked him for a bicycle, Dad told us, "I won't give you one, but I'll make it possible for you to earn the money to buy one." I was eight years old, and my brother was ten. Dad bought 100 calendars for us to sell for 35 cents each. After we paid Dad back, we made a 50% profit — a grand total of $17.50. The Western Flyer at the store cost exactly that amount. It took almost two months for us to sell all those calendars, but when the last one was sold, we experienced tremendous satisfaction when we rolled that bike out of the store.

A LEGACY CONTINUED

To a significant extent, we are products of our past — for good or ill. How our parents and grandparents handled adversity, and how they communicate those stories to us, profoundly shapes our lives. My father certainly didn't have an easy life, but he rose to every challenge with courage and integrity. The legacy I've briefly outlined blends the twin rivers of education and ministry, but more than that, my life has been shaped by the exemplary character of my grandfather and father. These men saw opportunity when others saw problems. They took bold action when others might have cowered in fear, and they imparted strength and hope when others who endure similar experiences may have crumbled into despair.

With such a rich family history, it's no surprise that the purpose of my life is consumed with a deep devotion to God and to educating young people. Every fiber of my life resonates with these elements because I see the tremendous power of blending academic excellence and character development. The church's impact was never meant to be relegated to an hour in a building on Sunday morning. Its

> *Every fiber of my life resonates with these elements because I see the tremendous power of blending academic excellence and character development.*

influence should permeate every aspect of community life. And the same heart and the same purposes have captured my children. The legacy of my grandfather and father lives in them and, I trust, will have a powerfully positive influence on their children and grandchildren as well.

My family's legacy, however, isn't limited to flesh and blood relatives. In the past few years, I've found countless men and women across the country who share my commitments and need a little help to make their dreams become a reality. These men and women, from every corner of the nation and every walk of life, yearn to leave an imprint on their own children and the kids in their communities. They want to create environments of love and excellence, places where mutual respect is the foundation for academic and personal excellence. When I have the opportunity to assist them, I'm well aware that I'm helping them create a long-lasting culture that will have a profoundly positive impact on children for generations — and the legacy will continue to expand.

The impact of our hard work to create charter schools isn't demonstrated by reams of documents and approvals by the state. The most gratifying moments of my life occur when I look into the faces of children who feel loved and are thrilled to learn new lessons each day. I hear their excited chatter about their school projects, I see them respond to the love of their teachers, and I hear stories of amazing transformations from rebellion to hope, and from withdrawal to happy engagement. I don't have to be in the halls of our schools each day. Our gifted administrators and teachers certainly don't need my help. But I need to be there for my sake, to remind me why I work hard to help people open new schools. To look at their faces and hear their voices tells me it's worth it — well worth it. I tell the children, "I'm so happy you're at our school. Do you know that you can be anything you want to be?" I love to go to our high schools where young people feel confident enough to look me in the eye and give me a firm handshake. They aren't confused about who they are, and they aren't ashamed about things they're hiding from adults. They are becoming whole, healthy young men and women full of purpose and hope for the future.

Some days, the strain of running multiple schools weighs on me. Every year, more parents want to enroll more students, and I want to provide every possible place for students to attend our schools. This pressure to expand causes additional stress, and I often need a strong dose of healthy perspective. On these days, I make sure to get out of my office and walk the halls of our schools, talking to students, listening to their chatter, and looking through the windows of the doors of classrooms to see today's version of a dream come true.

YOUR LEGACY, TOO

It is, perhaps, the most hackneyed phrase to say that today's students are tomorrow's leaders. This statement, however, can be taken as either a warning or a promise. If our schools fail to prepare students with a powerful combination of academic excellence and character development, the future looks bleak indeed. But if students have thrived in loving, stimulating school environments, taught by teachers who believe they are fulfilling their own dreams every day and supported by parents who have taken responsibility for their children's future, young men and women will be ready to lead our country with strength, wisdom, and courage. Success occurs when preparation meets opportunity. I believe that charter schools offer the best hope to prepare students to meet the opportunities and challenges they'll face the rest of their lives.

All of us are searching for significance, and in my opinion, there's no greater significance than protecting children and providing them with the resources they need to craft meaningful lives.

All of us are searching for significance, and in my opinion, there's no greater significance than protecting children and providing them with the resources they need to craft meaningful lives. Many people devote their energies to acquire money and possessions to leave their children an inheritance, but an inheritance can be easily lost or quickly consumed. A legacy, however, endures. It's not tangible, but it has the power to shape generations of children.

Today, I can honestly say that I experience a deep, abiding sense of fulfillment. When I look at the faces of the children in our classrooms and hear stories from their parents and teachers, I know my life has significance — and there's nothing better than that.

If you've read through this book, you obviously care very much about the legacy you're leaving to your children and the impact you want to have on your community. As you consider a possible role in establishing a charter school, I hope you grasp the significance your efforts can produce. You will pay a price for your commitment. You'll spend long hours of tedious labor, and you'll share your vision so often it will become second nature to you. But when you see the faces of children who lack quality schools, your heart will break. And when you eventually see the joy on those same faces when they feel safe and stimulated in a charter school environment, your heart will sing.

One of the truths about me is that I need to know that I've given my best and I've given all I have to give. My efforts to establish charter schools has given me a deep, abiding sense of satisfaction because I've been able to give my very best to every school we've started, and at the end of every day, I know I haven't held anything back. If you devote yourself to a charter school, you can feel the same way each day.

One of the most gratifying legacies you can leave is your impact on teachers who move from traditional public schools to a charter school. These dear men and women love children, and they long to make a difference every day, to shape young lives and point them toward a hope-filled future. Many of them feel terribly frustrated in public school settings, but when they teach in charter schools, they come alive again. If you start a charter school, teacher after teacher will thank you for restoring their hope and giving them the opportunity to touch students' lives in a meaningful way.

Another part of the legacy you can leave behind, one that will endure for generations, is the impact you'll have on parents. Today, many young parents simply haven't seen good models of parenting skills. They're doing the best they can, but they know they need help. A charter school can, through seminars like the ones we conduct at Life Schools, impart insight and skills so that parents can raise their children more effectively. When confusion and frustration are replaced with love and logic, amazing things happen — in the child, in the parents, in the community, and for generations to come as good parenting is replicated.

All of us bring our unique, God-given abilities and experiences to every opportunity in life. We can't do everything, but we can do something. We need to pray, reflect, and consider how we can make the most profound impact on others. I've chosen to devote myself to establish charter schools, but I don't make that assumption for everyone else. Find a cause that captures your heart, one that keeps you up at night because you want to right wrongs and make a difference in the lives of people. To have an impact, you don't need to have a particular background, education, or set of experiences. These can help, but they aren't as important as a rare and valuable trait: heart-felt desire to touch people's lives.

> *We can't do everything, but we can do something.*

Andy Chester

My first encounter with Life School came seven years ago when I was coaching basketball in a neighboring town and the Life School Lions played our team. As soon as the Life School students entered the gym, I knew that there was something different – and something special – about these young men and young women. They carried themselves with distinction and played with enthusiasm.

For the next few years, my school played Life School in a variety of sports, and each time our students, coaches, and fans went away with an even greater respect for Life School and its students and coaches. This impression stayed with me, and when the opportunity came to join the Life School family, I couldn't pass it up.

Starting an athletic program from scratch at the Red Oak campus was a daunting task, but the leadership and support of the administration, and the patience and understanding of the students and parents, made the transition go smoothly. The enthusiasm that first year was unforgettable, and the excitement continues to grow each year as we add more participating students.

My position as a campus athletic coordinator and coach the first two years at Life School enabled me to get to know our students and their parents and provided the opportunity to use athletics as a valuable tool for teaching the wonderful life lessons that sports can offer. The concepts of hard work, dedication to others, and sacrifice for the good of the group are just a few of the extraordinary character qualities that we impart to our students (and their parents as well).

With my new position this year as district athletic director, my opportunities for being hands-on with our students and parents has changed somewhat, but I now get to work with the coaches at both campuses, and I get to know even more students and their parents.

Being a part of Life School has changed me both personally and professionally. I've worked at several schools in my 20-plus years in education, and at each school, we talked about how our school should be a family. At Life School, however, the idea of being a family isn't just talk. The teachers' love for the students is evident each day. The staff's love and respect for each other is obvious in how we treat each other. And the administration has shown our staff how to be effective, compassionate, and hard-working leaders—traits that we can pass on to our students, and through them, to our world.

Andy Chester
Life School Athletic Director

Barbara Calhoun

Life School is certainly more than buildings filled with books, chairs, and technology. It is, in my opinion, a lifeline to the families who have chosen to entrust the educational needs of their children to educators who are not only passionate about what they teach, but are also dedicated to the well being of those whom they teach.

While standing between the walls in the building and trying to decide which story I wanted to share (there are so many good ones), I began to reflect on the many situations that have helped make Life School, in my opinion, one of most unique learning institutions in Dallas. As I looked at the walls, I wondered what truths were held beneath the drywall, mud, tape, and sometimes, chipped paint. I imagined that if these inanimate objects could articulate all they had seen and heard, they would, without doubt, tell stories that are as diverse as the small hands that lean against them for support each day. It was at that point that I knew I would share a story that inculcated in me a true love and respect for servant leaders.

After teaching in private education for nearly twenty years, I was privileged to be asked to join a remarkable team of educators and administrators at Life Charter School. Since the school was in its infancy, many programs, including a hot lunch program, were not yet established, which resulted in students being asked to bring lunches from home. Although many of the children brought tasty meals, some weren't as fortunate, so the principal, along with the assistant principal and counselor, decided to step briefly from the role of administrators to stop and feed children who brought no food.

One day while waiting for my students to enter the cafeteria, I witnessed something that has been, for me, a life changing experience because it exemplified the true meaning of love and dedication. The administrators decided to purchase, possibly from their own resources, a supply of bread, peanut butter, jelly, chips, and drinks to ensure that every hungry child was fed. These ladies weren't satisfied with merely purchasing the food; they also took time from a very hectic schedule to make sandwiches for these children. And as if buying and making the lunches weren't enough, they remained in the cafeteria until each child from each grade level received a lunch.

A Chance at Life

As I stood on that particular day, waiting patiently for my class to be seated, a gentleman accompanied by another administrator walked into the cafeteria and asked to meet with the principal. I later learned that the gentleman was a very prominent individual who, in another situation or school, would have gotten an immediate response to his request, but the principal simply responded that she would be happy to meet with him later, and she continued the task of serving the children. I don't remember the gentleman's name or his response to being denied an immediate interview with the principal. I only remember the smile and contentment on the faces of the children being served.

Some people in other schools may not have agreed with the principal's decision that day, but I thought it was one of the greatest acts of humility I had ever witnessed. Many years have passed and many things have changed, including a lunch program that ensures that all children, including those without resources, are able to eat. The children waiting to be served that day may have forgotten or perhaps never noticed the gentleman, but they, the wall and I have never forgotten the women who sacrificed their time and resources to make certain that every child who entered those cafeteria doors was fed.

Barbara Calhoun
Associate Principal (3-6)/Dean of Discipline, Life School Oak Cliff

Christy Murphy

Life School has left an imprint on my life forever. I am eternally grateful for Dr. Wilson and his vision for education, and our communities will forever be changed because of him and his amazing support team. The central office employees and school staff have servant's hearts and are truly using their talents every day. Dr. Wilson's powerful team has impacted many people in numerous ways. They have impacted my life as an educator and as a parent.

I was hired five years ago by the campus principal, Joseph Mena and Dr. Wilson. Dr. Wilson meets with every person so that he can share his heart and allow them to understand his vision. He speaks with such passion about the school and his staff that you are easily drawn to him and want to be a part of his team. The teachers are positive role models that encourage good character along with academic excellence to help the students strive to become leaders. At Life School, I'm surrounded by people that have a passion for teaching and a true love for children. I embrace the tally system and the parenting program that is unique to Life School. Life School understands that a parent is also an educator. The parents and teachers form a strong link that is the foundation of Life School's success.

Recently, I've been able to see Life School from a parent's point of view. My daughter, Aubrey, started Kindergarten. I know that she is in a safe environment that will push her to reach her full learning potential. Life School is a place that will help her develop good character that will be instilled in her forever. My perception of Life School is strengthened as I see the love that my daughter has for school and her teachers. Aubrey was a shy girl before entering Kindergarten, but she has grown more confident. Now I can see that she is not afraid to ask questions. She feels safe and loved — which is a blessing for any parent to see.

I'm proud that my daughter and I both have built trusting relationships with the staff, parents, and students of Life School. Not only has Life School touched my heart, but also I thank the teachers and administrators for taking such great care of my precious daughter.

She and I are eternally grateful for Dr. Wilson. As a parent and an educator, I'm proud to be a part of the Life School family.

Christy Murphy
Special Programs Coordinator
Life School Red Oak

Character Traits

In our schools, we teach, model, and emphasize these qualities so that they become ingrained in the lives of our students.

RESPONSIBILITY—proving you can be trusted with what is expected of you.

INDIVIDUALITY—discovering who you are meant to be so you can make a difference.

COOPERATION—working together to do more than you can do alone.

COMPASSION—caring enough to do something about someone else's need.

DISCIPLINE—doing what you need to do even when you don't feel like it.

SERVICE—lending a hand to help someone else.

HONESTY—watching what you say and do so others will trust you.

FRIENDSHIP—sharing special times with someone you trust and enjoy.

ENDURANCE—sticking with what you started even when it gets tough.

WISDOM—knowing what God wants you to do and choosing to do it.

CONTENTMENT—deciding to be happy with what you've got.

TRUST—putting your confidence in someone you can depend on.

KNOWLEDGE—discovering something new so you can be better at whatever you do.

DETERMINATION—deciding it's worth it to finish what you've started.

GRATITUDE—letting others know you see how they've helped you.

GENEROSITY—making someone's day by giving something away.

RESOURCEFULNESS—using what you have to get the job done.

FAIRNESS—making sure that everyone is treated equally.

HOPE—believing that something good can come out of something bad.

CONVICTION—standing for what is right even when others don't.

OBEDIENCE—trusting those who lead you by doing what you're asked to do.

FAITH—deciding to trust in what you can't see because of what you can see.

FORGIVENESS—deciding that someone who has wronged you doesn't have to pay.

LOVE—choosing to give someone your time and attention, no matter what.

INITIATIVE—seeing what needs to be done and doing it.

RESPECT—responding with words and actions that show others they are important.

UNIQUENESS—learning more about others so you can know more about yourself.

PEACE—proving that you care more about others than winning an argument.

ORDERLINESS—arranging things to make your day easier.

KINDNESS—showing others they are valuable by how you treat them.

COURAGE—being brave enough to do what you should do even when you're afraid.

JOY—Finding a way to be happy, even when things don't go your way.

PATIENCE—waiting until later for what you want now.

HUMILITY—putting others first by giving up what you think you deserve.

SELF-CONTROL—choosing to do what you should do, not what you want to do.

HONOR—letting people know you see how valuable they really are.

ABOUT THE AUTHOR

Dr. Tom Wilson, founder and superintendent of Life School, began a career in education in 1966. He has served as a speaker, pastor, and director of private schools, and he worked with organizations that have founded both national and international schools. Dr. Wilson married Brenda Kaye Mangrum in 1966, and four sons were born to them from 1969 through 1980.

Dr. Wilson organized Life Schools of Dallas in 1989 to train adults who were jobless and without employable skills. Homeless housing, medical care, and job placement services operated successfully. Activities for youth and children were provided, and they were very successful in terms of the hundreds of youth involved. However, the crowds came and went, and Dr. Wilson was dissatisfied to see only a small percentage of persons whose lifestyles were permanently changed.

Gang warfare erupted on the streets of Dallas in 1993. Dallas became the murder capital of the nation with the highest percentage of murders per capita of any United States city of 100,000 people or more. Dr. Wilson envisioned a tuition-free school to teach and train the children before they get in trouble.

During the next five years, Dr. Wilson read scores of textbooks addressing educational philosophy and successful school paradigms, and raised funds to provide resources to start a school. In

1997, he worked on a charter school application from the Texas Education Agency (TEA).

Skilled educational lawyers, notable educators, and community leaders all worked together with Dr. Wilson to complete the extensive documentation required in the application. The TEA charter was granted on March 6, 1998, and Life School became a tuition-free, open-enrollment charter public school on August 12, 1998.

Since its modest beginning, Life School's enrollment has soared from 266 students to over 3,100 students in the current year. All school campuses received Gold Performance Acknowledgements from the TEA this fall, based on Spring 2008 test results. Life School student composite test scores exceeded those of many surrounding public school districts on the Texas Assessment of Knowledge and Skills (TAKS) tests last year.

Dr. Wilson is also the founder and president of National Charter Consultants, providing assistants to individuals and groups who want to start charter schools in their communities.

Leaders of Life School with Ms. Mavis Knight, Member of the Texas State Board of Education

About National Charter Consultants

National Charter Consultants, (NCC) helps entrepreneurial leaders and community groups start charter public schools. Tom Wilson, Ph.D., is founder and president, He leads an outstanding team of consultants to work with leaders to *start* and *grow* charter public schools toward excellence in education.

NCC offers specific services designed for people interested in starting a charter school or converting a private school to a charter public school.

- Dr. Tom Wilson comes alongside your launch team to provide an assessment of suitability.

- Next, the start-up planning process begins, including assessments of the political climate, area demographics, facilities assessments, next steps, etc.—identifying potential barriers and providing action plans.

- NCC assists the founder and launch team in navigating each step of the process, including:

    — Complete information about charter public schools
    — Nurturing community/political resources to apply for a public school charter

- Guidance in applying for public education charter (Forty of the fifty states, Puerto Rico, and the District of Columbia have passed charter school legislation)
- Creating your school's board to be a financial and leadership resource
- Educational and methodological plans for the delivery of effective education
- Business and financial planning
- Structuring successful operating systems
- Preparations dealing with the political, legal, and public facets of operations
- Dealing with discipline
- Developing the campus culture
- Learning to motivate parental involvement: the untapped potential in education
- Planning in-service staff training
- Parent/Teachers, booster clubs, and other community support organizations
- Building your leadership team
- Recruiting excellent staff and teachers
- Dealing with governmental bureaucracy

To learn more:
- Visit the Life School website: www.lifeschools.net

- Visit the NCC website: www.nationalcharterconsultants.com

- Visit The Oaks Fellowship website and link to Dr. Tom Wilson: www.theoaksonline.org

To Contract NCC Services for You or Community Stakeholders, Consider These Options:

COACHING OPTION #1
"Go-to-Meeting," "SKYPE," or Satellite Seminar
- Receive a copy of the story of Life School, *A Chance at Life*, seminar materials, and brochures.
- Consultation includes:
    — One person, one-on-one with Dr. Wilson
    or
    — Three-hour seminar with an unlimited number of participants

LEVEL OF COMMITMENT: Investigation of the Possibilities

COACHING OPTION #2
Tour of Life School campuses, Seminar and a Q & A time with Dr. Wilson and his team of consultants.
- The leader receives a copy of *Charter Schools and Public Policy*, Dr. Wilson's doctoral dissertation
- Each participant receives a copy of *A Chance at Life*, seminar materials, and brochures.
- One person (if he returns leading a group, he receives a free pass)
    or
- Up to six participants (the leader receives a free pass)
- Additional fee for each additional person with group

LEVEL OF COMMITMENT: LOW—Exploration

COACHING OPTION #3
Dr. Wilson and the team of consultants custom design a meeting with your launch team at your location. They will assess your facilities, staff requirements, and legal obligations after the interactive

meetings with stakeholders and provide a report within 30 days.

LEVEL OF COMMITMENT: MEDIUM—Implementation and Planning

COACHING OPTION #4

Dr. Wilson facilitates planning and implementation of the application process petitioning for your Charter Public School. The process creates the school conceptually in application documents to qualify for an educational charter. The point person of your team will have access to Dr. Wilson via cell phone, "Go-To-Meeting" appointments, and "SKYPE" telecommunication conferences. Your approved team captains may also have access as needed.

LEVEL OF COMMITMENT: HIGH—Detailed planning process

Contact NCC for a fee schedule for each coaching option.

www.nationalcharterconsultants.com

TO ORDER RESOURCES

A Chance at Life
$24.99 each
Dr. Tom Wilson's story of
Life Schools

My First One Hundred Years
$20.00 each
Frances Eastes Wilson,
Dr. Wilson's mother and
centenarian authoress
1908–

Charter Schools and Public Policy
$75.00 each
Dr. Wilson's Doctoral Dissertation,
University of Texas at Dallas: the
history and process of establishing
charter schools

TO ORDER:

Go online:
www.nationalcharterconsultants.com

Write:
Tom Wilson, Ph.D.
National Charter Consultants
6 Remington Ct.
Red Oak, TX 75154

Phone:
(972) 617-3536

Email:
twilson@theoaksonline.org